D0801215

FIX IT GOOD
HOME

Mike Lawrence

FIX IT GOOD
HOME

HOW TO CARRY OUT YOUR HOME FIXES LIKE A PROFESSIONAL

TED SMART

This edition produced for
THE BOOK PEOPLE LTD
Hall Wood Avenue, Haydock
St Helens WA11 9UL

© The Ivy Press Limited 2004

All rights reserved. No part of
this publication may be reproduced,
stored in a retrieval system, or
transmitted, in any form or by
any means, electronic, mechanical,
photocopying, recording or otherwise,
without prior permission in writing
from the publisher.

THE IVY PRESS LIMITED
The Old Candlemakers
Lewes, East Sussex BN7 2NZ

Creative Director PETER BRIDGEWATER
Publisher SOPHIE COLLINS
Editorial Director JASON HOOK
Design Manager SIMON GOGGIN
Senior Project Editor REBECCA SARACENO
Designer JANE LANAWAY
Illustrations COREL MULA,
PETERS & ZABRANSKY AGENCY

Printed and bound in China

1 3 5 7 9 10 8 6 4 2

Every effort has been made to ensure that the instructions given in this book are accurate.
However, they are provided for general information only, and you should always read and
follow any manufacturer's instructions and, where appropriate, seek professional advice.

Contents

Introduction

The day you move into your first home is the day when you discover DIY. As time goes by, the list of improvements, maintenance and repair jobs that need doing inside and outside the house will slowly get longer and longer... unless you get a grip on them from the beginning. Many of these jobs are too small to hand over to the professionals, who will be delighted to re-surface your drive or replace your roof but can rarely be bothered to come and repair a dripping tap. So when something needs fixing, the answer is to fix it yourself.

To find out how to do this, you could buy yourself a blockbuster DIY manual. However, most of these simply offer too much information, which can seem daunting and off-putting, or perhaps you can't find what you want quickly and easily amongst all the detail, or else you get sidetracked into reading about something you didn't need to know anyway.

What you need is *Fix It Good: Home*. It contains all the information you'll ever need to do all those easy fixes yourself, in one compact volume that's small enough to keep in your toolbox. Everything in it is made simple. You'll find easy-to-follow instructions, step-by-step illustrations, tools and materials checklists and lots of tips from the experts, all designed so that you can see at a glance exactly what to do and how to do it. It will banish your incipient DIY phobia for ever.

Fix It Good: Home starts with the basics. It tells you briefly about your home's electricity and plumbing systems and your gas supply, so that you know how to turn things off in a household emergency. Then it fixes you up with a basic toolkit so that you can get started on all sorts of everyday jobs. The book begins with the little fixes that help to make a room complete, from putting up pictures and mirrors to hanging curtains and blinds. Decorating gets the full treatment, because that's what most homeowners do most. Doors, windows, floors and stairs are not forgotten – each of them has its own section of the book – and there are also some ideas for making the most of storage space around the house. The indoors section finishes with a look at some of the plumbing and electrical jobs that take little time to fix, yet cost a fortune if left to the professionals.

Outside the house, *Fix It Good: Home* cleans and repairs brickwork and rendering, sorts out minor roofing problems and takes a straightforward and practical look at exterior decorating. It tells you how to lay and repair paving and concrete, build a simple timber deck, install an outside tap and clear a blocked drain – perhaps the ultimate DIY nightmare, but often surprisingly easy to fix if you know how.

Fix It Good: Home is small enough to fit in your toolbox. It contains all the DIY you'll ever need, and nothing more.

BASICS

Electrics

There are several things you ought to know about your home from the day you move in. And if you don't know them yet, you need to find out about them now. They'll help you cope in emergencies and carry out all sorts of everyday fixes. Let's start with the electrics.

Consumer unit

Every home has an electrical nerve centre. In a modern house, it's a one-piece box of tricks called a consumer unit. This contains a main on-off switch that controls the power supply to the whole house.

It also contains special switches called miniature circuit breakers (MCBs), one for each light and power circuit in the house. The MCB switches itself off if you overload the circuit or there's an electrical fault. Once the fault is fixed, you switch the MCB back on to restore the power.

The consumer unit may also contain another safety feature – a residual current device (RCD), which detects current leaking to earth and shuts off the power immediately, preventing you from receiving an electric shock.

❶ Consumer unit

❷ Main on/off switch

❸ Miniature circuit breakers (MCBs)

❹ Residual current device (RCD)

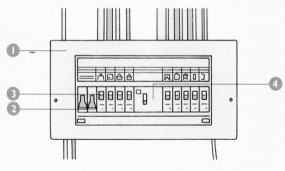

Fuses

Fuses are vital protective devices that cut off the power supply if you try to take too much current from a circuit. Never replace a blown fuse with any other metallic object to restore the power supply; your action could cost a life.

Fuse boxes

Older homes have a consumer unit containing fuses rather than MCBs – again, one for each circuit in the house. The fuse may contain a cartridge or a length of special fuse wire. Each is designed to melt and switch off the current if there's an overload or an electrical fault. A melted ('blown') fuse has to be replaced to restore the power (*see page 251* for more details).

Electricity meter

A meter sited close to the consumer unit records how much electricity you are using, in units called kiloWatt hours (kWh for short). One kWh is the amount of electricity used in one hour by a 1kW (1000 watt) electric fire, or in 10 hours by a 100-watt light bulb. Older meters have dial readouts; modern meters have digital ones.

Fuses

Fuse ratings are:

1 5-amp = light circuit

2 15-amp = water heater circuit

3 30-amp = power circuit

4 45-amp = cooker circuit

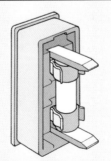

cartridge fuse

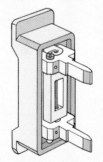

rewirable fuse

Gas

If your house has a gas supply, make sure you know where your gas meter and the main on-off lever are situated. They will probably be in an under-stairs cupboard in an older house, and in a wall-mounted cabinet in a newer one.

The gas

If you use mains gas, the incoming underground supply pipe will enter the house via a main on-off control lever and a gas meter. Use this lever to turn off the supply in the event of a gas leak, rotating the lever until it is at right angles to the pipe. The meter records the volume of gas you use, and your supplier converts this into kWh before calculating your bill.

❶ Incoming supply pipe

❷ On/off lever

❸ Flexible connector

❹ Supply to house appliances

❺ Pressure controller

❻ Display

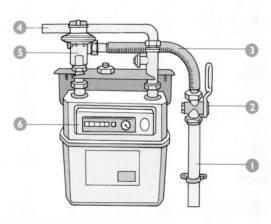

The plumbing system

Your house plumbing system consists of two main parts – the water supply and the waste disposal system. If you understand a little about how they work it will help you to cope with any plumbing emergencies that may arise.

The water supply

Your house water supply arrives through an underground pipe. After it enters the house, it travels upwards, either feeding cold taps and WC cisterns as it rises (a direct system), or supplying a big storage tank in the loft from which cold taps and WCs are then supplied (an indirect system). See page 224 for more details about plumbing systems.

There will be a main stoptap on this pipe at ground level, controlling the water flow into the system. Make sure you know where this is, and

 check regularly that it will turn freely should you need to use it in an emergency.

Old houses

In old, unmodernized houses there may be no indoor stoptap. Instead the water flow into the house is controlled by an underground stoptap, located in a small chamber near the property boundary. If this is your situation, it is a good idea to get an indoor stoptap fitted.

Waste pipes and drains

Used water from the house runs via slim waste pipes and a large-diameter soil pipe down into the underground drains and on into the local sewer network. Each waste pipe is fitted with a U-shaped trap that contains water and prevents drain smells from entering the house. These can be dismantled to allow access to the waste pipes if you have to clear a blockage.

You can trace where the drains run by locating the underground manholes (inspection chambers) between the house and the property boundary.

Hand tool basics

Even if you don't plan on doing much fixing around the house, there's a handful of tools no home should be without. With these, you can hang a picture, undo a screw, drill a hole and cut a shelf down to size.

Claw hammer

A hammer drives nails, taps things into position and knocks things apart. If it's got a claw opposite the head, it will pull out nails and lever things away from other things – like lifting a damaged floorboard, for example. Pick one with a metal shaft and a comfortable moulded grip, with a head weighing 16 or 20oz (hammers haven't gone metric yet).

❶ Hammer head

❷ Claw

❸ Handle

Screwdrivers

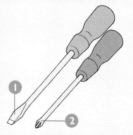

You'll find you can never have too many screwdrivers. Screws come in different sizes, and may have slotted or cross-shaped recesses in their heads, so you need drivers for both types. The best value is a to buy a box, containing two or three sizes of flat-tip screwdrivers and two or three for cross-head screws. Add a small flat-tip electrician's screwdriver for electrical repair jobs.

❶ Flat-tip blade

❷ Cross-point blade

Pliers

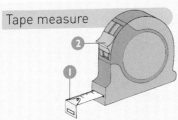

A pair of pliers will do all sorts of basic gripping jobs, and can also be used as a makeshift spanner for nuts and bolts as well as a wire cutter. Buy a pair with insulated plastic handles.

❶ Gripping jaws

❷ Wire cutter

❸ Handles

Junior hacksaw

This small steel-framed saw is designed to cut metal (bolts, pipes and so on), but will also cut plastic (such as a curtain track) and even small pieces of wood. You replace the blade when it gets blunt or breaks.

❶ Steel frame

❷ Replaceable blade

Tape measure

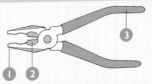

Lots of jobs around the house involve measuring things, so you'll need a steel tape measure. Buy one that's 3m (10ft) long, with metric and imperial markings so it can act as a converter between the two systems. It's handy to have a lock that holds the tape when it's extended.

❶ End hook

❷ Tape lock

Spirit level

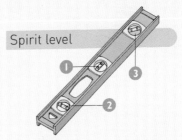

This tool tells you if things like shelves are level (horizontal), and also if they're truly vertical – like a fence post, for example. Get the bubble between the marked lines in the vial and you've set the horizontal or vertical precisely. Buy one 300mm (12in) long to begin with.

❶ Level vial

❷ Vertical vial

❸ Adjustable vial

Trimming knife

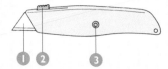

This is used for all sorts of cutting and trimming jobs, and has replaceable blades. Some have fixed blades, but one with a retractable blade is safer to carry around. You can also fit special blades for cutting sheet flooring material, thin wood and even metal.

❶ Blade

❷ Blade slider

❸ Handle fixing screw

Staple gun

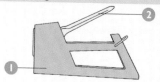

This handy tool fires staples like those in a desk stapler and can make all sorts of light-duty fixings – securing carpet underlay, for example, or fixing fabric to a roller blind. It leaves your other hand free to hold whatever you're fixing. Buy one capable of firing a variety of staple types.

❶ Staple magazine

❷ Operating handle

Adjustable spanner

You'll find an adjustable spanner useful for tightening or undoing things that are too big for your pliers – the nuts on plumbing fittings, for example, which may need tightening to stop a leak. Buy the crescent pattern with its offset head, in a size that will open to about 30mm (1¼in).

❶ Movable jaw

❷ Adjustment screw

Cartridge gun

This sounds like a specialist tool, but it's incredibly useful for applying fillers, mastics and adhesives now that so many of these products come in standard cartridges. You just slot in the cartridge and squeeze the handles to extrude the product like toothpaste.

❶ Cartridge holder

❷ Trigger operated plunger

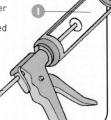

Cable and pipe detector

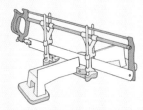

This battery-powered tool detects the presence of cables or pipes that are buried beneath wall surfaces. Use it before banging nails or driving screws into walls, so you don't hit something you shouldn't. Most will also detect floor joists and the studs inside partition walls.

Sensor

Mitre saw jig

For jobs too small for the power jig (*see page 23*), it's useful to get one of these. This all-in-one mitre saw jig will make straight or angled cuts in a wide variety of wooden mouldings and sections. It can make perfect mitred (45°) cuts on skirting board, picture rails and the like as well.

Straight-edge

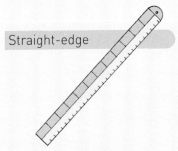

A steel straight-edge (ruler) is handy for guiding your trimming knife when you're cutting things, and for testing that surfaces like tiled walls are flat. Get one about 1m (3ft) long, with metric and imperial markings on it.

Try square

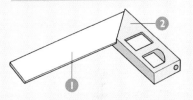

This has two main uses. It helps you to mark cuts squarely across pieces of wood, and lets you check that interior and exterior angles are right angles – for example, when you're assembling flat-pack furniture.

❶ Blade

❷ Stock

Bradawl

This little tool is used to make pilot holes for small screws in wood and other materials. Choose one with a chisel tip rather than a point. For larger screws, you'll need to drill pilot holes instead.

❶ Point

❷ Handle

Chisels

Chisels are used for a variety of trimming and paring jobs, and come in widths from 6mm (¼in) upwards. They have to be sharpened (with oil on an oilstone) regularly. Buy them as and when you need them.

❶ Oilstone

❷ Oil can

❸ Narrow chisel

❹ Broad chisel

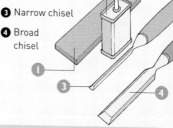

Nail punch

This steel tool has a cup-shaped recess in its tip, and is used with a hammer to punch nail and pin heads below the surface so you can fill the recess and hide the fixing.

❶ Tapered tip

❷ Square head

Clamps

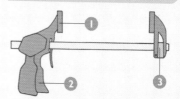

Clamps hold things together and are invaluable for holding pieces of wood steady while you cut or drill them. Buy a pair of quick-release clamps with jaws that open to about 75mm (3in).

❶ Movable jaw

❷ Trigger handle

❸ Fixed jaw

Surform planer

This tool shapes wood rather like a cheese grater, and is very useful for jobs like easing a sticking door or rounding off the corners of a piece of wood. You can buy different shapes, and the blades can be replaced when they get blunt.

❶ Handle

❷ Replaceable blade

Pin hammer

This lightweight hammer will take over from your big claw hammer for driving small nails in awkward corners. Use the wedge end to start the nail while you hold it in place, then switch to the flat head to drive it home. Use with your nail punch for hiding nail heads.

❶ Wedge

❷ Head

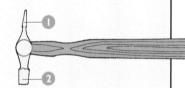

Portable workbench

You'll find a small fold-away workbench invaluable for all sorts of jobs. You can take it to wherever you're working, and use it for sawing, drilling and assembling things – it can also act like a giant vice. You can hang it on the garage wall when you've finished.

❶ Jaws worktop

❷ Jaw adjuster

❸ Frame

❹ Footrest

❺ Folding legs

Power tool basics

Power tools save time and effort, and can give better results than their hand tool equivalents. Your basic tool kit should include a cordless drill, a jigsaw and a sander, plus a selection of drill bits, saw blades and abrasive sheets to fit them.

Cordless drill

You can take a cordless drill anywhere without needing a mains power supply. The drill comes with its own battery charger, and many are supplied with a plastic storage case as well.

TIP

Store your cordless drill indoors, rather than in a garage. The batteries will gradually lose their ability to accept a recharge if they are stored in very cold conditions, and the temperature in an unheated garage or shed can drop to zero during cold weather.

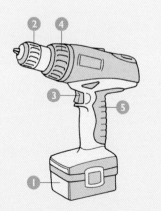

Features to look for

❶ 12 or 14.4 volt battery plus a spare

❷ Keyless 10mm (⅜in) chuck

❸ Variable speed (including reverse for removing screws)

❹ Hammer action (for drilling masonry walls)

❺ A comfortable fit in your hand

Mains drill

Consider adding a mains drill if you do a lot of DIY that involves drilling masonry. Its faster drilling speed and extra power will speed up this type of work. Look for a drill with a power rating of at least 500 watts, two speed settings, hammer action and a 13mm (½in) keyless chuck. You will also need an extension lead.

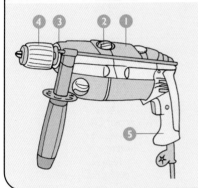

Features to look for

❶ Power rating of at least 500 watts

❷ Two speed settings

❸ Hammer action

❹ 13mm (½in) keyless chuck

❺ A comfortable fit in your hand

Drill bits

You will need a twist drill bit for making small holes in wood and metal. Buy a set in sizes 1–10mm (1⁄6–1⅜in). Add a countersink for recessing screw heads, screwdriver bits for slotted and cross-head screws, and two or three masonry bits – the most useful sizes are 6, 7 and 8mm (¼–⅝in) – for making holes in solid walls. You may need special bits too, such as a tile bit; a screw sink – which drills pilot and clearance holes and a countersink in one go. A hole saw cuts large holes in man-made boards and plastic sheet.

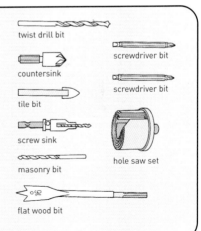

twist drill bit

screwdriver bit

countersink

screwdriver bit

tile bit

screw sink

hole saw set

masonry bit

flat wood bit

Sander

A power sander takes all the hard work out of sanding wood and man-made boards, and can also be used to smooth plaster and fillers. The simplest type is the orbital sander (1), which takes rectangular sheets of abrasive. Eccentric or random-orbit sanders use sanding discs. Both are ideal for general sanding of flat surfaces. Detail or delta sanders (2) use small triangular sanding sheets and are ideal for finishing work in tight corners. Palm sanders (3) are smaller and lighter versions of the orbital sander.

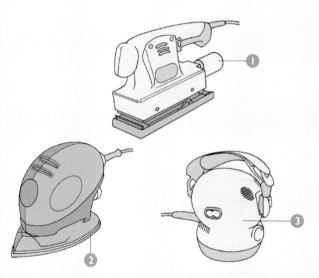

Abrasives

Most sanders use abrasive sheets coated with aluminium oxide, which come in fine, medium and coarse grades. Make sure you have the right size of sheet to fit each model.

Features to look for

❶ Dust bag or dust extraction facility (needs perforated abrasive sheets)

❷ Quick-fit abrasive pads held in place by Velcro attachments.

Jigsaw

A mains-powered jigsaw (which is also known as a sabre saw) drives a short blade up and down through a baseplate, which you rest on the material you are cutting. It will make straight and curved cuts in wood and man-made boards up to about 50mm (2in) thick, and you can fit a variety of different blades for cutting metals, plastics and even ceramic tiles.

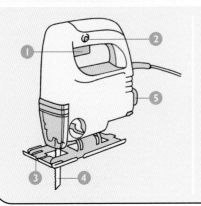

Features to look for

❶ Variable speed control

❷ Lock-on switch for continuous use

❸ Adjustable baseplate for making cuts at angles up to 45°

❹ Manual (tool-free) blade change

❺ Dust extraction facility (allows tool to be connected to a vacuum cleaner).

Jigsaw blades

❶ Wood-cutting blades are available for coarse, medium and fine cutting; these will also cut through plastic.

❷ Blades for metal have much finer teeth.

❸ Blades for cutting ceramic tiles are abrasive-coated.

Buy wood blades in sets and others as you need them.

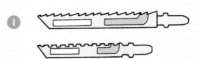

Fixings

You won't get far in the DIY world without doing some fixing – joining things together, attaching them to other things and so on. Here are some of the essential fixings you'll need:

Nails

Nails are pointed steel fixings with heads you drive in with a hammer. Use them when you want a quick fixing that probably won't need undoing. There are lots of different types for different jobs, but you're likely to need only a few.

Wire nails

The most useful nail is the oval wire nail. Drive it with its long axis parallel to the wood grain to reduce the risk of splitting. Lost-head types are easier to punch in for an invisible fixing. The most

Masonry nails

These hardened nails are used to fix wood directly to solid walls. Always wear goggles when driving them in in case they break. They're very hard to remove once in place. Sizes range from 25 to 100mm (1 to 4in).

Flooring nails

Traditionally, cut nails were used to fix floorboards to their joists, and they're still the best type for the job. You can use ring-shank nails instead because they resist being pulled out very well. Common sizes for both are 50 and 75mm (2 and 3in).

useful sizes are 25, 50 and 75mm (1, 2 and 3in) long. Use round wire nails for fixing frameworks where the nails will be out of sight, such as in partition walls and similar structures.

Panel pins

These slim pins fix thin panels and trim to thicker wood. Hardboard panel pins have diamond heads that you can punch into the board surface. Common sizes for panel pins are 15 to 50mm ($^5/_8$ to 2in).

Screws

Screws are threaded metal fixings that make a strong pull-resistant fixing, yet are easy to remove if required. Most modern screws are threaded all the way up; others have a smooth shank section next to the head.

slotted countersunk

cross-head

Screws are put in with screwdrivers, which fit into a recess in the screw head. The recess may be a plain slot or a cross-shape. Use cross-head (Pozidriv) screws for everyday fixings because you can drive them with a cordless drill or screwdriver. Use slotted-head screws for fixing hardware such as door and window fittings.

slotted head   Pozidriv head

Screw heads may be (A) countersunk, (B) round or (C) raised-and-countersunk. Use countersunk screws for general woodwork, sinking the head flush in a countersunk hole drilled in the wood. Use round and raised-head screws for fixing hardware such as door and window fittings to wood.

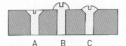

A   B   C

Wall fixings

You can't generally drive screws directly into walls or ceilings, unless they're timber-framed and you know where the framing is. Instead you need a fixing device to suit the wall.

For solid masonry, you drill a hole using a masonry drill bit and push in a plastic wallplug to line the hole. This expands to grip the sides of the hole securely as you drive in the screw. For most fixings, you need just two sizes of plug, each requiring a different size of drill bit.

large plug   small plug

For hollow walls and ceilings, you need different fixings for different loads. For lightweight fixings, use plastic or metal plugs, which you screw into a pilot hole in the plasterboard, ready to take a fixing screw. For medium-weight fixings, use a plastic anchor or a spring toggle. For heavy fixings, use metal anchors. All these grip the inner face of the board as you drive in the fixing screw.

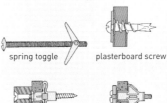

spring toggle   plasterboard screw

plastic anchor   metal anchor (open)

Safety basics

DIY isn't dangerous in itself, but there are lots of ways of having an accident and injuring yourself if you're not careful and sensible. Here are some danger areas to watch out for.

Ladders and steps

More deaths and injuries are caused by falls from ladders and steps than by any other DIY activity.

• Set ladders up at the correct angle. That means having the bottom of the ladder 1m (3ft) out from the wall for every 4m (12ft) of ladder height. Never use a ladder as a horizontal work platform.

• Rest the foot of the ladder or steps on firm level ground, or on a stout board packed up so it is level. Tie the top of the ladder to the building if you can.

• With an extending ladder, make sure at least three rungs overlap. Extend the ladder before you raise it into position. Use a ladder stay to hold the top of the ladder clear of the gutter at eaves level.

• Don't climb a ladder with your hands full. Wear a tool belt or apron, and fit a tool tray to the ladder so you can put things down safely as you work. Use the top four rungs only as a hand-hold.

• Don't lean out too far. You may lose your balance or cause the ladder to slip sideways. Keep your hips within the line of the ladder sides, and hold on with one hand whenever possible.

• Set steps up so you're facing the work. Check that the sides are locked in position. Never stand on the top step.

❶ Ladder stay

❷ Foot rest

❸ Ladder stabilisers

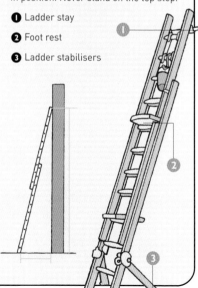

Tool safety

• Use the right tool for the job. Don't improvise: you'll probably damage the tool, and you may hurt yourself too.

• Keep your hands behind the direction of cut when using bladed tools – especially trimming knives and chisels. Fit blade guards before storing them.

• Sharpen or replace blunt tools. They are more likely to cause an accident than sharp ones because you have to force them to do their job.

• Read power tool instructions before using the tool for the first time. Make sure blades and bits are properly fitted. Never by-pass or remove safety guards.

Materials safety

Some DIY materials may burn skin, injure eyes, or give off unpleasant or inflammable fumes. Always read the instructions on the packaging, and wear the appropriate safety equipment.

Electrical safety

• Remember that electricity can kill. Unplug power tools and appliances before trying to clean or adjust them.

• Use a cable and pipe detector to check for hidden cables or pipes in walls and floors before drilling holes or driving in nails.

• Plug power tools into a socket outlet or adaptor containing a residual current device (RCD).

• Don't tackle electrical work unless you know what you are doing. Make sure the power is switched off at the mains before starting such work.

Safety gear

Wear the appropriate safety gear to protect yourself from dust, noise, flying debris and falling objects. You might need:

1 Safety goggles or spectacles

2 Disposable face mask

3 Ear defenders or ear plugs

4 Gloves (leather or fabric for general use, pvc for handling chemicals)

5 Safety helmet

INDOORS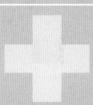

Pictures and mirrors

Pictures add a personal touch to any room, whether it's the heirloom Renoir, a group of family photographs or a couple of cheap prints, while mirrors will reflect light into dark corners. But there's more to hanging them than simply banging a few nails into the wall.

you will need

→ basic tool kit
→ picture hooks and pins *or*
→ screw-on hooks *or*
→ mirror plates (for heavy pictures) *or*
→ S-hooks for use with picture rails

See Hanging mirrors (*pages 33–35*) for methods of hanging pictures using mirror plates.

Picture hooks

❶ A single-pin metal picture hook is adequate for most pictures

❷ Use four-pin plastic hooks for lightweight pictures, tiles and plates

❸ Heavier pictures may need a two-pin hook *or*

❹ A screw-on hook *or*

❺ Two or more mirror plates

Fixing picture hooks

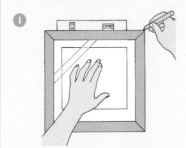

Hold the picture where you want it, and level it with a small spirit level on top. Make a light pencil mark on the wall behind each top corner. Make another mark midway between these two.

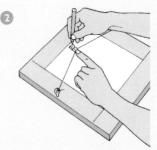

Place the picture face down, fit the hook and push it up so the cord or wire is taut. Mark the position of the top of the hook on the picture. Measure the distance between the top of the hook and the top of the frame.

Transfer this measurement to the wall, making a mark at this distance below the centre mark you made in step 1.

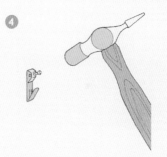

Hold the picture hook up to the lower mark and drive in the pin. The hook will ensure that it goes in at an angle.

Hanging heavy pictures

1

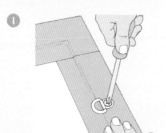

Screw a D-ring to each side of the frame, about a third of the way down. Measure the distance between them.

2

Mark the ring positions on the wall and fit screw-on hooks to the wall to match the ring spacing.

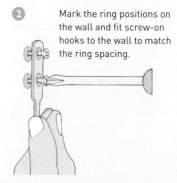

3

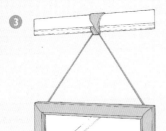

Use S-hooks to hang pictures from picture rails. Fit decorative chain as an alternative to picture wire or cord.

See Hanging mirrors (*pages 33–35*) for methods of hanging pictures using mirror plates.

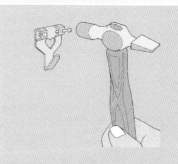

TIP

Use a two-pin hook for larger pictures, especially on a plasterboard wall. Make sure the hook is level. On a masonry wall, drive in one pin all the way first, then align the hook and hammer in the other pin.

Hanging mirrors

How you hang a mirror on a wall depends on whether it's plain, or has screw holes in it or a wooden frame. You also need to take account of the mirror's weight – large framed mirrors can be surprisingly heavy.

Mirror fixings

Choose the hardware to match the mirror you're hanging.

❶ Use mirror screws for mirrors with pre-drilled holes.

❷ Use corner plates *or*

❸ Sliding clips for plain mirrors; clips can fix round and oval mirrors as well as square or rectangular ones.

❹ Use mirror plates for hanging heavy framed mirrors (and heavy pictures too).

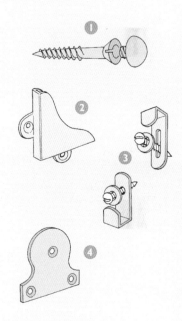

TIP

Do not position a mirror above a mantelpiece if you are in the habit of lighting a real or fuel-effect fire in the fireplace. Anyone standing in front of the mirror runs the risk of inflammable clothes catching fire.

you will need

→ basic toolkit
→ domed or capped mirror screws *or*
→ mirror corners *or*
→ mirror clips *or*
→ mirror plates

Using mirror screws

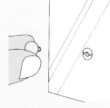

❶ Hold the mirror up, check that it's level and mark the screw positions on the wall. Drill and plug the holes.

❷ Hold the mirror in position and drive in the screws. Don't over-tighten them or you will crack the mirror. Finally, fit the domes.

Using corner plates

❶ Stick a plate to each corner of the mirror using masking tape.

❷ Hold the mirror up and mark the screw hole positions on the wall. Drill and plug the wall.

❸ Fix the bottom plates first, then the top ones, and remove the tape.

TIP

In bathrooms, fit a rubber tap washer on each screw, between the mirror and the wall. This will allow air to circulate behind the mirror and will help to stop it misting up.

Using mirror tiles

Mirror tiles are stuck in place with small adhesive pads. It is very difficult to get an even reflection when sticking the tiles to a plastered wall surface, which is rarely perfectly flat. Instead, stick the tiles to a panel of MDF first, then hang the tiled panel on the wall as for hanging an ordinary mirror.

An alternative to using adhesive pads is to stick the tiles in place using blobs of instant-grip adhesive. Apply a blob at each corner of the tile and press it into place on the MDF panel.

Using mirror plates

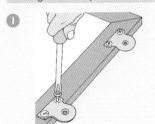

① Screw two mirror plates to the back of the top of the frame. Add another two at the bottom for a really heavy dressing mirror.

② Hold the mirror up and mark the screw hole positions on the wall. Drill and plug the wall.

③ Drive the fixing screws through the top plates first, then the bottom ones.

> When attaching mirror plates, check that the fixing screws will not penetrate the face of the frame, and that they will fit through the holes in the plates.

Using mirror clips

Hold the mirror up to the wall and mark where the clips will be placed against its edges.

Hold each clip to its pencil line, mark its screw hole and drill and plug the holes. Screw the clips in place – fixed at the bottom and sliding at the top.

Slide the top clips up, rest the mirror in the bottom clips and slide the top clips down to secure the mirror.

Putting up a curtain pole

Curtain poles are the simplest way of hanging curtains. You can choose poles in wood or metal, in a wide range of different finishes and styles. Make sure you select one that is long enough for the curtains to be drawn back clear of the window reveal.

1

Mark the positions of the pole brackets at the recommended spacings (including a centre bracket if required).

2

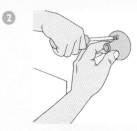

Hold one base plate up to its mark, pencil through the screw holes and drill and plug the holes. Screw it into place.

3

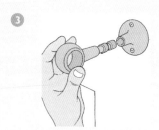

Fit the bracket into its base plate. Tighten the screw in the side of the socket with a hex key or screwdriver.

4

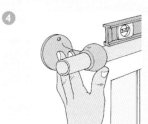

Fit the pole into the bracket, slip on the other end bracket and use a spirit level on the pole to set it level.

Curtain pole kit

Design details vary, but the pole and brackets shown here are typical. If you are hanging full-length or heavy lined curtains, it is a good idea to substitute longer screws and wall plugs for those supplied in the kit, for a secure fixing.

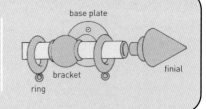

base plate

finial

bracket

ring

 5

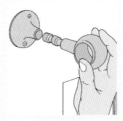

Mark the screw holes for this base plate, drill and plug the wall and screw it in place. Add the bracket as before.

 6

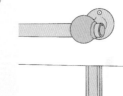

To fit a centre bracket, slide the pole out of one end bracket and add the centre bracket. Mark and fix it as before.

 7

Slide the pole out of each end bracket in turn and feed on the rings. Keep two rings to fit on the pole ends.

8

Centre the pole in the brackets and tighten the locking screw on top of each bracket. Fit the end finials.

Putting up a curtain track

Curtain tracks come in a wide range of styles, plain or corded and with clip-on valance rails so you can add a decorative pelmet to match (or contrast with) your curtains. Choose one that's about 600mm (24in) wider than your window opening.

1 If necessary, cut the track down in length. On corded track, remove the pulley casing and shorten that end. Re-centre the master carriers on the track.

2 Make a faint horizontal pencil line on the wall, then mark the bracket positions along it. Position the outer brackets 25mm (1in) in from the ends of the track.

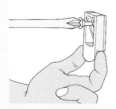

3 Mark screw holes and drill and plug the wall at each bracket position. Screw on all the brackets.

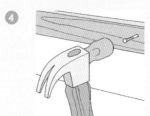

4 If you can't drill into a concrete lintel, fix a slim timber batten to the wall with masonry nails and fit the brackets to it.

Curtain track kit

The kit will contain everything you need to fit the track. However, if you are hanging full-length or heavy lined curtains, it is a good idea to substitute longer screws and wallplugs for those supplied, to guarantee a secure fixing.

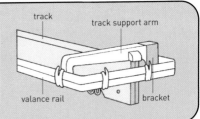

track   track support arm

valance rail   bracket

⑤

Clip a track support arm into each bracket. You can unclip them and lift off the track for future decorating.

⑥

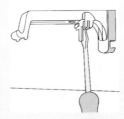

Slide a track support bracket and locking lever on to each arm, push it back and tighten the locking screw.

⑦

Offer up the track, locate the groove over the nibs on the locking levers and rotate them to lock the track in place.

⑧

Cut the valance rail to length, bend the ends back and snap on the hooks. Fit the rail to the track support arms.

Putting up a roller blind

Roller blinds are one of the cheapest ways of dressing your windows. They come as complete kits to fit standard windows, and it's easy to cut one down in width to fit a non-standard window or to hang inside the window reveal.

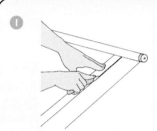

If you need to reduce the width of the blind, unroll it and cut the fabric with a sharp trimming knife and steel ruler.

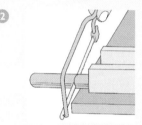

Cut the roller core to match the reduced fabric width. Use a hacksaw to cut a metal core and file the end smooth.

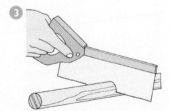

Some blinds are supplied with fabric and a separate wooden roller. Cut the roller to width first, then the fabric.

Fold over 20mm (⅞in) at one end of the fabric and either tack it to the wooden roller or fix it with a staple gun.

Roller blind kit

The kit will contain everything you need to fit the blind. Decide where you intend to position the blind – on the frame itself, inside the window opening or on the wall above it – before selecting the width you need.

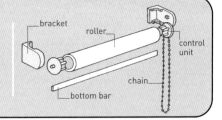

Labels: bracket, roller, control unit, chain, bottom bar

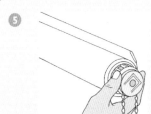

⑤ Fit the chain-operated control unit to one end of the roller and the free-spinning axle unit to the other end.

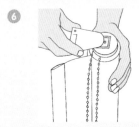

⑥ Slide the control unit into its bracket, but don't snap it fully home. Fit the axle unit into the other bracket.

⑦ Hold the blind in position against the frame and use a bradawl to mark the fixing hole through each bracket.

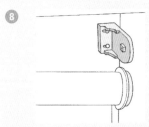

⑧ Screw the two brackets to the frame at the marks made in step 7. Then clip the roller into place and test it.

Putting up a Venetian blind

A slatted Venetian blind is perfect for windows where you want to adjust the amount of light coming in at different times of the day, as well as be able to close or open it. You can choose blinds with wooden slats, or coloured plastic or metal ones.

Venetian blind kit

The kit contains everything you need to fit the blind, which is usually installed within the window reveal. Wooden and plastic types can be cut down in width, but others must be made to measure. You may also need to shorten the blind to fit a shallow window.

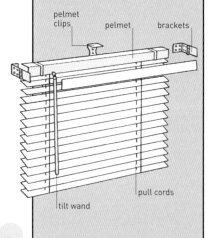

pelmet clips   pelmet   brackets

pull cords

tilt wand

Reducing the blind width

①

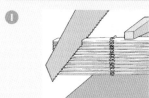

To reduce the width of a wooden blind, clamp the slats together and trim them at each end with a panel saw. Sand the cut ends smooth.

②

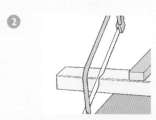

Ease the header bar away from the slats and cut it to the same width as the blind slats. Use a junior hacksaw if the header bar is plastic or metal.

Fitting the blind

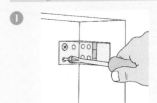

1

Fit the end brackets to the window frame. Hold each in place, mark the screw holes and screw on the brackets.

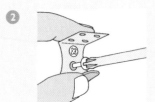

2

Add one or more intermediate brackets to the frame for blinds that are over 1200mm (4ft) wide.

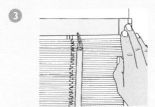

3

Fit the header bar into the brackets and close the flaps to secure the bar. It rests on any intermediate brackets.

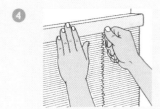

4

Attach the pelmet clips to the header bar and snap the pelmet into place to hide the end brackets.

Shortening the blind

1 Lower the blind to the sill and prise out the buttons retaining the pull cords from the bottom bar.

2 Cut the knots, remove the bottom bar and slide out slats to shorten the blind. Allow one extra rung on the ladder cords and cut off the excess.

3 Replace the bottom bar in the lowest ladder rungs, then thread the cords back through the holes in the bottom bar and through the buttons.

4 Tie a knot in the cord below each button, tuck the cord ends into the holes in the bar and press in the buttons.

Putting up a corded blind

Corded blinds have fine cords attached to the bottom bar of the blind. They run up through eyelets on the back of the fabric to the header bar, and travel along it to one side of the blind. There they are attached to a pull cord that operates the blind.

Corded blind kit

The kit contains everything you need to fit the blind, which can be installed within the window reveal or on the wall above it. A blind fitted within the reveal may need cutting down in width. One fitted above the window should be approximately 150mm (6in) wider than the window recess.

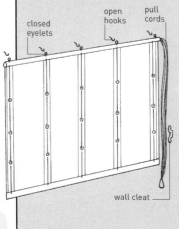

closed eyelets

open hooks

pull cords

wall cleat

Adapting the blind

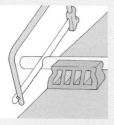

❶ If the blind is too wide to fit inside the window reveal, you can usually trim up to 25mm (1in) from each end of the head rail without having to cut down the fabric itself in width.

❷ Take care not to cut through the cords at the end where they are gathered.

❸ If the blind is too long for a shallow window, limit its drop by tying a knot in the pull cord. This will stop the lift cords from running back along the head rail as the blind is lowered.

Fitting the blind

Screw the closed eyelets into the pre-drilled holes of the metal head rail; drill pilot holes in a wooden rail.

 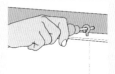

Get a helper to hold the blind up to the window frame, and mark through each eyelet with a bradawl.

Check that all your marks are level with each other and drill a pilot hole at each marked position.

Screw an open hook into each pilot hole until the thread is buried in the wood and each hook is vertical.

 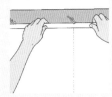

Lift the blind into place and fit the closed eyelets over the hooks. The pull cords should be on the inside.

 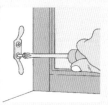

Screw the cleat to the inside of the window reveal, at the same side as the pull cord. Tie it off to hold the blind up.

Putting up a picture or dado rail

Timber wall mouldings at waist and head height can break up room walls and let you experiment with different decorations. A dado rail stops chair backs from marking the wall, while a picture rail lets you hang pictures and mirrors wherever you want.

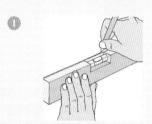

Decide where you want to position the rail and draw a horizontal guideline all around the room at that level.

Start work in one corner of the room. Drill and countersink holes in the rail at about 600mm (24in) intervals.

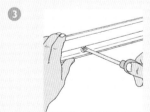

Hold the rail to the wall and mark the fixing holes. Drill and plug the holes, then screw the rail into position.

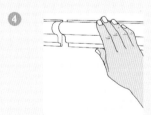

On long walls, butt joints between lengths of rail may open up. Cut 45° ends with a mitre saw jig, and glue them together.

you will need

→ basic toolkit
→ coping saw
→ timber mouldings
→ instant-grip adhesive

Fixing options

Never nail dado or
picture rails to the wall.
The best method is to
use screws and wall
plugs. You can also stick dado
rails to the wall with instant-grip adhesive, but
do not stick picture rails from which you plan to
hang pictures, in case the adhesive fails.

dado rail

picture rail

At internal corners, cut the end of the
next rail to fit over the face of the first
one. Draw the profile around an offcut.

Use a coping saw to cut the shaped
end of the second rail. Then drill and
countersink holes as before.

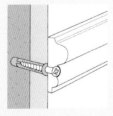

Spread adhesive on the shaped end
of the second rail, offer it up into the
corner and drive in the fixing screws.

Cut 45° mitres for external corners on
chimney breasts, using your mitre saw
jig. Glue, pin and fill the corner joints.

Putting up panel mouldings

One of the simplest ways of giving walls a different look is to break up the surface expanse with panel mouldings. They can be used to frame a picture or mirror, or will allow you to introduce areas of colour or texture to a plain wall.

you will need

→ basic toolkit
→ plaster mouldings
→ plaster adhesive
→ brown paper or
  newspaper
→ scissors
→ masking tape
→ filling knife
→ mitre box and tenon saw

Plaster mouldings

Panel mouldings are usually 25–50 mm (1–2in) wide. You can cut corner mitres or use pre-formed corners.

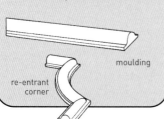

re-entrant
corner

moulding

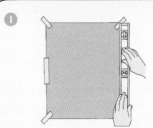

Plan the shape, size and position of your panel using brown paper and masking tape. Get it truly vertical.

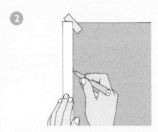

When you are happy, use a ruler and pencil to draw guidelines around the perimeter of the template. Remove it.

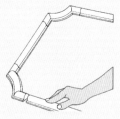

Take measurements from the template and cut the mouldings to length. Test the fit on the floor.

If using corner mouldings, stick the first one to the wall with adhesive, aligning it with the pencil guidelines.

Add an upright section of moulding next, and check that it is vertical. Trim away excess adhesive and fill gaps.

Continue adding corners and straight sections until the panel is complete. Check the verticals and horizontals.

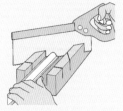

Cut 45° corner mitres if you prefer square or rectangular panels. Use a mitre box and a fine-toothed saw.

Painting the mouldings

Touch up the wall colour before you paint the mouldings. Then stick masking tape to the wall along both sides of the mouldings and paint with two coats of diluted emulsion paint. Thinning helps prevent the paint from clogging up the details of the mouldings. Remove the tape as soon as the paint has dried.

Decorating

Decorating covers a multitude of options, from giving the walls a quick lick of new paint to doing a full room makeover. Whatever level of work you plan to carry out, it pays to spend a little time considering all the options.

The doors

• **Painted or varnished?** Apply a fresh coat of paint or varnish (*page 70*) after preparing the surface (*page 60*) and attending to any minor faults (*page 136*). To complete the facelift, you could replace the door handles (*page 138*), fit new hinges (*page 140*) or even consider replacing the door entirely (*page 142*). Fit new architrave mouldings if the existing ones are old-fashioned or damaged (*page 144*).

• **Stained?** Apply a fresh coat of varnish (*page 89*) to retain the colour, or apply another coat of matching woodstain to enhance or deepen it (*page 88*). Alternatively, you can paint the door for a complete change of look (*page 70*).

The windows

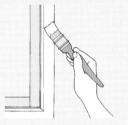

• **Painted or varnished?** As for doors, apply a fresh coat of paint or varnish (*pages 73–77*) after preparing the surface (*page 60*) and fixing any minor faults (*page 159*). Consider replacing the window fittings (*page 160*).

• **Stained?** As for doors, apply a fresh coat of varnish, stain (*page 88*) or paint (*pages 72–77*).

• **uPVC?** Wash down frames and sills with household detergent. Redecorating is not necessary, but uPVC frames can be painted if a colour change is required (*page 282*).

The ceiling

• **Painted plaster?** You can simply repaint it with a coat of fresh emulsion paint (*page 64*) after preparing the surface (*page 58*) and filling any cracks or damage (*page 98*).

• **Papered?** If your ceiling has been decorated with smooth lining paper (look for the tell-tale seams about 500mm [20in] apart), or with a relief wallcovering such as Anaglypta, you can apply fresh paint over it to freshen up the surface or change its colour (*page 64*). Attend to any lifting seams or ends first (*page 57*). You can hang a new wallcovering on a lined ceiling (*page 120*), but old relief wallcoverings must be stripped off if you want a change of design (*page 90*). You cannot paper over them.

• **Textured?** If your ceiling has a textured (Artexed) finish, you can repaint it as for painted plaster (*pages 64–69*). The finish can be removed (*page 59*) or plastered over – a job for a professional plasterer – if you no longer want a textured finish.

TIP

If you have a ceiling that is covered with polystyrene tiles, repaint it with emulsion paint – ideally a fire-retardant type. NEVER use any solvent-based paint, which will make the tiles more flammable.

The walls

• **Painted plaster?** As for ceilings, you can apply a fresh coat of emulsion paint (*page 64*) after preparing the surface (*page 56*) and attending to any cracks (*page 92*) or larger-scale plaster damage (*page 94*). You may need to apply two coats if you intend to change the colour dramatically.

• **Papered?** As for ceilings, you can repaint walls that have been decorated with smooth lining paper, woodchip paper or a relief wallcovering such as Anaglypta. Attend to any lifting seams or ends first (*page 57*). Patterned wallcoverings must be removed if you want a change of design or a return to plain walls (*page 90*).

• **Tiled?** Wall tiles are very durable, and may simply need cleaning and renovating to give them a new lease of life (*page 134*). You can tile over tiles (*page 218*) if you want a change of design, or paint over them if you just want a change of colour (*page 64*). Removing existing tiles will cause large-scale plaster damage, and will create a major job.

Other woodwork

• **Painted or varnished?** Prepare skirting boards and other timber mouldings (*page 60*), and repaint or revarnish them (*page 78*). Consider stripping old paint and repainting (or varnishing) if the existing surface is in poor condition (*page 84*). This applies to door and window paintwork too.

The floor

• **Keeping what's there?** Have carpets professionally cleaned. Wash and polish other floorcoverings, and carry out any necessary minor repairs (*page 168*).

• **Replacing the floorcovering?** Remove the old flooring (*page 172*), fix any structural faults (*page 174*) and lay a new floorcovering. You could consider woodstrip flooring (*page 186*), vinyl or cork tiles, ceramic or quarry tiles (*page 188*), sheet vinyl (*page 190*) or carpet (*page 192*).

• **Getting back to basics?** Consider sanding and varnishing floorboards (*pages 180–183*) or levelling (*page 184*) and painting a concrete floor.

Radiators and pipework

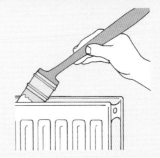

• **Painted?** Prepare painted metal surfaces (*page 62*) and then repaint them (*page 80*). Use radiator enamel rather than ordinary white gloss paint to reduce yellowing in future.

• **Bare?** Clean tarnished copper pipework with wire wool and then apply two coats of paint or radiator enamel. Apply clear metal lacquer if you want to keep the freshly polished look.

TIP

Paint radiators and central heating pipework the same colour as the room walls to make them blend in with the background. Modern all-surface paints will cope with the effects of heat better than ordinary emulsion paint.

Small furniture

• Move easily portable items to other rooms in the house. This includes side tables, stools, upright chairs, bedside cabinets, table and standard lamps – the list is endless.

Big furniture

• Things like sofas, big chairs, dining tables and beds are probably too big to take out of the room. Push them together in the centre of the room and cover them with dust sheets. Don't forget to take down the centre light fitting first (*see page 55*).

Storage units

• You may be able to slide freestanding wardrobes away from the wall you plan to redecorate without emptying them first. Don't try to shift display cabinets or bookshelves when they are loaded, though. Instead, empty them shelf by shelf into boxes, and take those out before trying to move the unit itself.

Wall-mounted units

• Empty these and unscrew them from their wall fixings. Leave the screws in the wall plugs so you can reuse the fixings afterwards.

Curtains

• Take down curtains and blinds, and unscrew curtain tracks; both will probably need cleaning. Leave the wall fixings in place for reuse.

Pictures

• Take down all pictures and mirrors. If you want to rehang them where they were, remove the hook, but leave the picture pin in place.

Floorcoverings

• **If they're staying** Cover all types of floorcovering with fabric dust sheets – old bed sheets and duvet covers are ideal. To help keep them in place as you work, use a wide-bladed tool, such as a filling knife or brick bolster, to tuck their edges underneath the skirting boards all around the room. Don't use plastic dust sheets. They're slippery, easily dislodged and potentially dangerous underfoot, and any paint splashes stay wet and get trodden everywhere. Fabric dust sheets soak up splashes and can easily be shaken free of debris for reuse time after time.

• **If they're going** Lift them before you start work. Discard old carpet underlay – it's cheap to replace, and new carpet deserves new underlay. You may have cork and vinyl tiles or sheet vinyl stuck to a hardboard underlay on timber floors, or directly to a solid concrete floor. Leave these if they are securely fixed; most types of new floorcovering can be laid directly over them.

Radiators and pipework

• **Leave well alone** Simply repaint them after preparing their surfaces (*page 62*). It is acceptable to paint or paper the walls behind them only as far as you can comfortably reach (or see).

• **Remove when necessary** The only time you need to remove radiators is if you have old wallpaper behind them that you want to strip. If you haven't tackled the job and don't have the right tools, call in a plumber to remove the radiators before you start and replace them afterwards. They will also need to check that the heating system has refilled properly, and that the control and isolating valves are set correctly.

Doors and windows

• Unscrew and remove door and window handles and catches. Wedge doors open and hold casement windows open with stiff wire wound around screws driven into the existing holes.

Ceiling lights

• Unscrew and remove pendant lampshades. This is a good opportunity to dust or wash them if they're being kept. Replace the light bulb with a brighter one for extra light while you're decorating. Remove other light fittings by turning off the power supply at the mains, unscrewing them from the ceiling and disconnecting the wiring. Then lift them down and set them aside for cleaning. Leave the removal job to an electrician unless you know what you are doing. Otherwise, simply enclose the whole fitting in a clear plastic bag tied with gardening wire.

Switches and sockets

• Apply masking tape to the edges of the faceplates if you're repainting. If you are stripping wallpaper, loosen their fixing screws and tuck a small plastic bag around the faceplate before retightening the screws. This will keep water out while you work.

Wall lights

• Turn off the power supply and unscrew the fitting from the wall. As with ceiling lights, disconnect the wiring and remove the fitting. Otherwise, just loosen the screws holding the light to the wall and enclose it in a plastic bag.

Burglar alarm sensors

• Switch off the system, unscrew these from the wall and cover each with a small plastic bag tied with wire.

TIP

Although you may be tempted to try, it is very difficult to redecorate a room without removing some (or all) of the furniture and taking down the fixtures and fittings. It may take time at the outset, but you will get on much more quickly with a blank canvas to work on.

Preparing walls for a repaint

The simplest redecoration you can do is to give already painted walls a fresh coat of paint. You can copy what's there to give the room a facelift, or experiment with a new colour scheme for a completely different look.

you will need

→ bucket
→ sponge or soft cloths
→ sugar soap or detergent
→ rubber gloves
→ dust sheets
→ sponge sanding block
→ paint scraper
→ 'lipstick' paper adhesive
→ tube of quick-setting filler
→ small filling knife

Washing down

Mix up a bucketful of sugar soap or detergent with hot water. Put down dust sheets and wash each wall. If the wall was painted with a glossy solvent-based paint, first rub it down with a wet sponge sanding block to key the surface. Allow to dry thoroughly before repainting.

Dealing with flaky paint

Remove any loose paint with a sharp scraper, then use a sanding block to smooth the edges of the hole.

Touch in the bare area with a little paint. This will prevent the hole from being visible when you repaint the wall.

Painted wallpaper

Your walls may be decorated with lining paper, woodchip or a relief wallpaper such as Anaglypta. All of these are intended to be painted once hung. Unless you plan to strip them off (*see page 90*), you may need to fix any minor faults before painting.

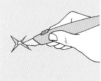

Slit any air bubbles with two cuts at right angles. Peel back the tongues and apply a little paper adhesive from a 'lipstick' dispenser. Press the tongues back to the wall for an invisible repair.

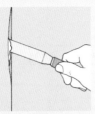

Stick down lifting seams by spreading paper adhesive from the dispenser on to a knife blade and inserting it under the edge of the wallpaper. Press the seam down to stick it back in place.

TIP

New plaster may produce a white powdery deposit on the surface, called efflorescence. It is caused by salt deposits, but it will eventually cease to appear. Brush it off when dry.

Hiding unwanted fixings

If you've taken down old fixtures such as curtain track and you plan to fit new ones, you will need to make new fixing holes and conceal the old ones.

❶ After removing the fixture, replace the screw in the wall plug and tap it with a hammer to push the plug deeper into its hole. Then remove the screw.

❷ As an alternative, insert the screw, but use pliers to pull the screw and plug out of the wall. Don't worry if you dislodge an extra bit of plaster.

❸ Squirt quick-setting filler from a tube into each hole, leaving it proud of the surface. Trim it off and sand it smooth when it has set hard.

Preparing ceilings

The ceiling is every home decorator's least favourite surface. Because it's overhead, decorating it is hard physical work, but this has to be done, and that means beginning with some basic preparation of the existing surface.

you will need

→ bucket

→ squeegee or mop

→ soft-bristled brush for textures

→ sugar soap or household detergent

→ rubber gloves

→ dust sheets

→ stain blocker

→ fungicide

→ textured paint remover

→ large paint brush

→ paint scraper

Dealing with stains

❶ Seal in stains caused by past plumbing leaks by spraying on a special aerosol stain blocker.

❷ Alternatively, paint over stains with any solvent-based primer or top coat. This will prevent the stain from bleeding through subsequent coats of emulsion.

Dealing with mould

After washing the ceiling, treat any areas discoloured with black mould by brushing on a solution of fungicide, or of household bleach diluted 1 part bleach to 5 parts water. Leave for 24 hours, then scrub off and rinse with clean water. Allow to dry.

Washing down

Mix up sugar soap or detergent as for walls, and put down fabric dust sheets. Use a squeegee mop to wash smooth or lightly textured surfaces, then rinse out the mop and wash the ceiling with clean water. Leave it to dry. Wash around light fittings by hand. Use a soft-bristled brush to clean deeply textured surfaces such as Artex, then blot them dry as best you can with old towels.

Textured finishes

If you have a textured ceiling finish such as Artex that you no longer want, you have three options for dealing with it.

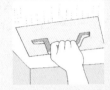

Use a hired steam stripper to soften the finish. Take care not to overdo the steam, or you risk damaging the plaster.

Apply a skim coat of finishing plaster over the texture. Leave this to a professional plasterer if you prefer.

As each area softens, scrape it off with a broad scraper and deposit the scrapings in a metal container.

Cover the finish by nailing up a new plasterboard ceiling surface. Mark the joist positions on the ceiling first.

Stripping textured paint

If steam stripping doesn't soften a textured finish, it may be textured emulsion paint rather than a true textured finish. You can remove this by brushing on special textured paint remover. Leave it to soften the paint for the recommended time, then scrape off the residue. Wear a cap, safety goggles and a face mask while doing this, and be warned: it's a long and messy job. You might prefer one of the above options instead.

Resteam any stubborn patches. Finish by sanding any remaining rough areas using a power sander.

Preparing woodwork

Woodwork is usually finished with paint that has a gloss or eggshell (satin gloss) finish. These paints were traditionally solvent-based, but now you can buy water-based equivalents that are easier and more pleasant to use.

you will need

→ bucket
→ sugar soap or household detergent
→ rubber gloves
→ sponge or soft cloths
→ wet-and-dry abrasive paper *or*
→ sponge sanding blocks
→ fine surface filler
→ plastic spatula or filling knife
→ fine glasspaper
→ knotting solution
→ wood primer
→ small paint brush

Washing down

Even if your paintwork is apparently in perfect condition, always wash it down before repainting it. If you do not, the surface film of dirt, grease and finger marks will prevent the new paint from adhering satisfactorily.

❶ Use sugar soap or detergent solution applied with a sponge or a soft cloth, then rinse off with clean water.

❷ Next, key the paint surface by rubbing it over lightly with wet-and-dry abrasive paper or a sponge sanding block. This will remove the surface gloss from the paint, giving the new paint a better chance of bonding to it. Use the abrasive wet, rinsing it out as necessary. Wipe off the paint slurry with a damp cloth and leave it to dry.

Minor blemishes

If bare wood is showing through, touch in the chip with wood primer. Apply extra coats to fill the hole.

If the surface is dented but unbroken, apply fine surface filler over the dent with a plastic spatula or filling knife.

When the filler has set hard, sand it smooth with fine glasspaper until it is flush with the surrounding surface.

If the paint is stained by resin bleeding from a knot in the wood, sand it back to bare wood and apply knotting solution.

Leave the knotting solution to dry. Then brush on one or two coats of wood primer over the bare wood.

If the wood grain is visible through the old paint, apply fine surface filler overall and sand it smooth when it has dried.

Preparing metalwork

In most homes, there is little metalwork on show that needs painting – mainly central heating radiators and pipework. Older homes may still have galvanized steel or aluminium window frames that will need repainting from time to time.

you will need

→ bucket
→ sugar soap or household detergent
→ rubber gloves
→ sponge or soft cloths
→ wet-and-dry abrasive paper *or*
→ sponge sanding blocks
→ fine wire wool
→ white spirit
→ rust-inhibiting primer
→ small paint brush
→ metal polish

Washing down

Prepare painted metalwork in sound condition as for woodwork (*page 60*), washing down the surface and then keying it ready for the new paint.

Tackling rust spots

The galvanized steel used for most domestic central heating radiators will rust if the metal is exposed to the air. Areas of rust may also indicate the presence of pinhole leaks in the radiator, especially along the side and bottom seams, caused by internal corrosion.

❶ If you find any rust spots, remove them by rubbing them with wire wool moistened with a little white spirit.

❷ Use a wire brush attachment in a power drill for more extensive rust patches. Then apply metal primer.

TIPS

Make sure that there is no build-up of old paint on radiator control and bleed valves, and on in-line isolating valves on pipes supplying taps and WC cisterns. Remove any that you find using a sharp knife and wire wool, to allow the valves to be operated freely when required.

Prepare aluminium windows for painting by rubbing with fine wet-and-dry abrasive paper moistened with white spirit until you expose bright metal. Wipe the surface, then apply a coat of zinc phosphate metal primer.

Preparing metal windows

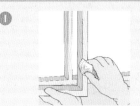

❶ Use wire wool or a wire brush attachment in a power drill to remove rust from galvanized steel frames.

❷ Wash the area with white spirit, then apply rust-inhibiting primer to the bare metal to prevent rust from recurring.

Preparing copper pipes

Copper pipework develops a dull brown colour if left unpainted. Any minor plumbing leaks lead to the creation of green deposits called verdigris, and should be cured (*page 239*) before the pipework is painted.

❶ Remove surface discoloration and degrease the surface by rubbing it with wire wool moistened with white spirit.

❷ Remove any metal particles and loose debris by wiping the surface with a dry cloth, to leave it ready for painting.

Cleaning brass

Brass is used indoors mainly for door furniture, and is generally coated with a clear lacquer finish to prevent it from discolouring. If this lacquer is damaged, unscrew the affected item and brush on liquid paint stripper to remove the lacquer. This will also remove any paint inadvertently applied during past repainting of the door. Then clean the exposed metal with brass polish, and wipe the cleaned surface with white spirit to leave it ready for a fresh coat of clear lacquer.

Painting walls and ceilings

The simplest and quickest facelift for any room is a quick re-paint – applying a fresh coat or two of emulsion paint over an existing painted surface. All you have to do is choose the colour to use and how to put the paint on.

you will need

→ paint
→ paint brushes *or*
→ paint roller and tray *or*
→ paint pads and tray
→ dust sheets
→ masking tape
→ small stepladder

TIP

Your paintwork may have a variety of small chips and dents caused by everyday wear and tear, and these will show through the new paint unless they are dealt with first.

Masking off

However steady your hand, you'll find it difficult to get perfectly straight edges where your new paintwork meets the ceiling and other surfaces, such as door and window frames, skirting boards and light switches. Masking these edges with masking tape before you start decorating will save time as you work, and will give your work a neat and professional finish. Use tape at least 25mm (1in) wide. Press the tape down firmly along its length to prevent paint from seeping under it, and remove it as soon as the paint is touch dry.

Providing safe access

Do not be tempted to improvise access equipment by standing on chairs or resting boards on furniture. Such arrangements are dangerous, and a fall could injure you and spill paint everywhere. Buy, hire or borrow the proper equipment for the job.

Hiring equipment
Visit your local plant hire shop and ask for advice on hiring the access equipment you need. You can hire things by the day, weekend or week.

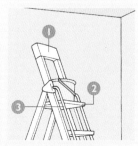

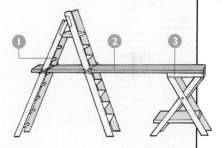

❶ At the very least, you will need a stepladder to reach your ceiling and enable you to work comfortably.

❷ Choose a stepladder with a top platform on which you can rest your paint tin or roller tray.

❸ A hand grip will allow you to steady yourself as you work.

❶ An alternative is to set up a work platform using a stepladder and another support.

❷ Rest a scaffold board between two stepladders or other sturdy supports.

❸ You can also hire trestles and staging from local plant hire firms.

How much paint?

① Most emulsion paints will cover roughly 12sq m (130sq ft) per litre when applied over existing paint.

② To estimate how much you need, measure the height and perimeter of the room and multiply the two figures.

③ Disregard doors and small windows.

④ Buy enough paint to complete the job with a little left over – buying more later from a different batch may result in a slight, but noticeable, colour difference.

Painting walls

Using a brush for walls

If you are a brush fan, you will need a 75 or 100mm (3 or 4in) size for the main painting. Larger brushes cover faster, but are tiring to use, particularly for the inexperienced painter. Add a 25mm (1in) brush for cutting in at edges and around other obstacles.

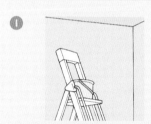

Start painting at the top right-hand corner of each wall if you are right-handed, and vice versa. Aim to cover about 1sq m (10sq ft) at a time.

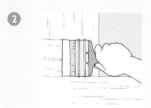

Apply paint in parallel vertical strips, then brush horizontally to blend the strips. Finish with vertical strokes.

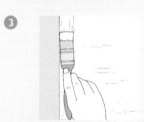

After completing the main area of wall, use your narrow brush to cut in around the edges, up to the masking tape.

Using a roller

If you prefer a roller, use one with a short-pile sleeve. You will also need a narrow brush for cutting in around the edges of each wall.

Use a longer-pile sleeve for painting rough surfaces such as relief wallpaper and textured finishes.

Pour paint into the roller tray and load the sleeve evenly by running it up and down the sloping part of the tray.

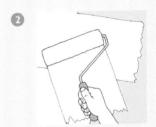

Apply paint in up-and-down and criss-cross passes. Reload the roller as necessary to paint the next area.

Using a paint pad

Choose a large pad for the main areas and a slim one for cutting in at edges.

You can buy pads individually or as a kit, usually containing a large and medium wall pad, plus one or more smaller pads for painting details and touching in at edges and corners.

Pour paint into the tray and load the pad by running it over the built-in roller. Take care to load the pad evenly.

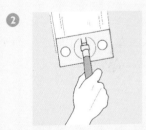

Apply paint in overlapping bands to ensure good coverage. Reload the pad as necessary, then cut in at edges.

Painting ceilings

Using a brush

Most people paint ceilings white to reflect the maximum amount of light into the room. However, colour can be very effective, especially in tall rooms where the effect is to make the ceiling seem lower.

Use a 100mm (4in) brush. Start at the edge nearest the window and work in bands towards the opposite wall.

TIP

Because you are painting above your head, it is a good idea to wear a pair of safety spectacles to guard against getting splashes of paint in your eyes. It is also worth using non-drip paint, rather than the traditional runny type, to minimize the risk of splashing.

Cutting in

It is not necessary to mask the ceiling perimeter because any slight inaccuracies will not be noticeable from ground level. All you need to achieve good results is a steady hand and a good eye.

Cut in the narrow band all round the perimeter of the ceiling after painting the main area. Work quickly, so the main area blends with the edge band.

Unscrew ceiling rose covers and let them slide down the pendant flex so you can paint right up to the baseplate. Make sure the power is off.

Using a roller

Many people who happily use a roller for painting walls baulk at using one on a ceiling. Used correctly, a roller will cover a ceiling in far less time than a brush, and so long as the sleeve is not overloaded there is little risk of getting splashed with paint. You will have to cut in with a brush round the ceiling perimeter and around any light fittings (*see page 68*) before you start.

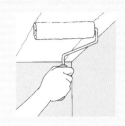

Use a 180mm (7in) roller. Start next to the window and apply paint in broad parallel bands, merging the wet edges.

Try using an extension pole fitted into the roller handle. This allows you to work from floor level, but it can be tiring.

On ceilings decorated with Artex or textured wallpaper, use a long-haired roller sleeve to paint into the relief.

TIP

To stop work during painting, wrap the roller sleeve in a plastic bag such as a shopping bag or a freezer bag to stop the paint from drying out. Squeeze the bag tightly round the sleeve to exclude air.

Painting a door

Doors get more wear and tear than any other part of a room, so they need painting in a tough and easy-to-clean finish. Most people choose a gloss or eggshell finish – usually solvent-based, although water-based products are now available.

you will need

→ paint
→ paint brushes
→ screwdriver
→ masking tape
→ door wedge
→ dust sheet

Before you start

Unscrew and remove the door handles from an interior door, and all the fittings from an exterior door. It is worth applying strips of tape over hinges (unless they have been painted over in the past) and over the faceplates of latches and mortise locks. Use a door wedge to prop the door open while you work.

See pages 78–79 for painting door frames and architraves.

Painting techniques

1 Always aim to paint one face of a door in a single session. If you stop part-way, you will find that the edges of the two painted areas will not blend together and will remain noticeable even when the paint has dried.

2 When painting a wooden door, always try to apply the paint parallel to the direction of the wood grain. You will notice that the top, centre and bottom rails of a panelled door have the grain of the wood running horizontally.

3 Avoid paint build-up on the door edges by finishing your final brush strokes towards the edges.

Painting a panelled door

This is the trickiest type of door to paint well, because of the many different edges and corners that are created by the panelling.

1 Paint the mouldings around the first panel with a 25mm (1in) brush or an angled cutting-in brush.

2 Paint the first panel, taking care not to let paint build up in the corners. Repeat steps 1 and 2 for the other door panels.

3 Paint the top, centre and bottom rails in turn, applying the paint in horizontal bands parallel with the wood grain.

4 Paint the centre vertical sections (called muntins) between each pair of door panels.

5 Paint the two outer vertical sections (called stiles) to complete the job. Finish with light vertical brush strokes.

6 If the door has different colours on each face, paint the latch edge of the door to match the face that opens into the room, and the hinge edge to match the other face.

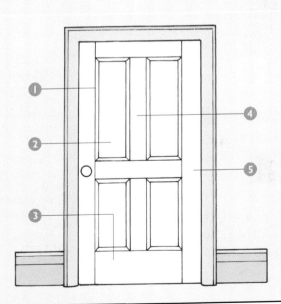

Painting a flush door

1 Divide the door face into eight imaginary squares.

2 Paint each one in turn, starting at the top right-hand corner and working across and down the door.

3 Work quickly, blending each wet area into the next to avoid visible joins as the paint dries. Finish each area with light vertical brush strokes.

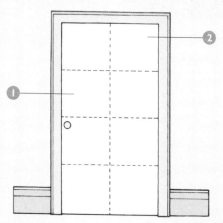

Painting a glazed door

Always use masking tape to outline the mouldings around the panes. Apply it about 2mm (⅛ in) in from the edge of the glass and leave it on until the paint is dry. Paint the mouldings first, then the rails and stiles.

Painting a front door

Start painting as early in the day as you can, to ensure that the new paint is hard before evening, when you need to replace the door furniture and close the door. Be aware of the security implications of having your front door open all day: it is best to wedge the door slightly ajar when you have finished painting, and to erect some sort of barrier inside it to prevent anyone from entering uninvited.

Painting a casement window

Hinged casement windows take time to paint, because of the many different surfaces involved. It is a good idea to organize your decorating so that you can paint the inside and outside of the window on the same day if possible.

you will need

→ paint
→ paint brushes
→ screwdriver
→ masking tape
→ stiff wire stay

TIP

Remove self-adhesive foam draught-stripping from the window before you start painting. Use white spirit to get rid of traces of old adhesive. Apply new draught-stripping all round when the paint has dried.

Before you start

Unscrew and remove the window catches and stays.

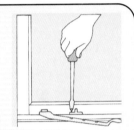

①

Drive a screw or nail into an existing screw hole on the casement and frame, and use a length of stiff wire (from a coathanger, for example) to link the two and make a temporary stay.

②

Wash the edges of the opening casement and the rebate in the frame to remove dirt, cobwebs and other debris that has built up over time.

③

Masking off

The paint film should extend onto the surface of the glass by about 2mm indoors and out. This seals the bedding putty and provides a wipe-clean surface that discourages the growth of mould indoors. Outdoors, it prevents rainwater seeping in. Apply masking tape all round each pane, just inside the edge of the putty, so you can create a perfectly straight edge. Don't use a plastic paint shield for this; you will end up with more paint on the glass than if you worked freehand.

Painting sequence

Start early so the paint will have set hard by evening. Then you can replace the window fittings and close the window with no risk of it sticking. See pages 278–281 for information on painting the outside of the frame.

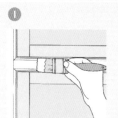  

❶ Paint the mouldings around the window panes first, plus any glazing bars between the panes on small-paned Georgian-style windows.

❷ Paint the indoor faces of each opening casement and top vent. Fit a wire stay to keep each open while the paint dries.

❸ Paint around any fixed panes, then tackle the rest of the frame and sill. Working from outside the house, paint the edges of each opening casement or top vent. Don't let paint clog up the drip grooves in the casement edges.

Painting a sash window

Sliding sash windows present quite a painting challenge, because of the difficulty in reaching some of the surfaces. It's also vital not to apply paint too thickly to the sides of the window frame, as this will cause the sashes to stick.

you will need

→ paint
→ paint brushes
→ screwdriver
→ masking tape

Before you start

Unscrew and remove the sash lock from the rails where the two sashes meet. Open the top sash fully and wash its top edge, and the top and sides of the frame to get rid of dust and other debris that could mar the paint finish. Close it and open the lower sash so you can wash the rest of the frame and the bottom edge of the lower sash.

Masking off

As with a casement window, take time to apply masking tape all around each pane, leaving a gap of about 2mm (⅛in) between the tape and the edge of the bedding putty.

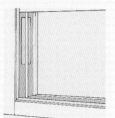

At each side of the frame, near the bottom, there will be a small rectangular panel called a pocket, which has to be removed to allow access to the weight compartments if you ever have to replace a broken sash cord. These are often painted over. However, it is better to prise them out, paint them separately and screw them back into place when the paint has dried. You will then be able to find and remove them easily in the future if needs be.

TIP

Tap two panel pins part-way into the bottom edge of the lower sash to prevent it from closing fully by accident while you are moving the sashes up and down to paint them.

Painting sequence

1

Push the bottom sash up as far as it will go and lower the top sash. Paint the top sash's meeting rail and as much of the sash sides and glazing bars as you can reach.

2

Reverse the positions of the sashes, but don't close them completely (see TIP on page 75). Paint the rest of the top sash. Avoid a paint build-up where the sash meets the sides of the frame.

3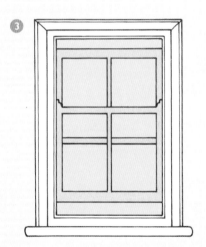

Paint the various surfaces of the bottom sash, including the top edge of the meeting rail.

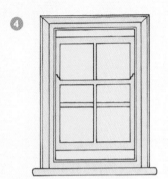

Paint the inner frame and its surrounding architrave mouldings, then the window sill.

Lower both sashes and paint the top and the exposed upper sides of the inner frame. Hold the sash cords aside so you do not get paint on them.

Finally, raise both sashes and paint the bottom and the exposed lower sides of the inner frame.

TIP

Use water-based paint for the sides of the frame. It will dry much more quickly, and the difference in the finish will be barely noticeable.

Painting other woodwork

Apart from its doors and windows, every room will contain an assortment of other woodwork that will also need painting. This includes door frames and architraves, skirting boards and possibly a picture or dado rail too.

you will need

→ paint
→ paint brushes
→ acrylic decorator's mastic
→ masking tape
→ knotting solution
→ paint shields
→ dust sheet

Before you start

One of the biggest problems with woodwork is that it tends to move, shrinking in dry weather and expanding slightly when it's damp and humid. This opens up cracks where the wood meets adjoining plaster surfaces, and ordinary hard filler simply crumbles away. The solution is to fill all such gaps with a flexible acrylic decorator's mastic before repainting. Run a thin bead of mastic along the joint, then smooth it with a wet finger.

Picture and dado rails

Use an old paint brush to dust the rail before you start painting. This is especially important for picture rails. Fill cracks and gaps with mastic and paint the walls above and below the rails.

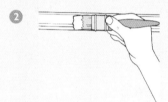

① Stick masking tape to the wall above and below the rail. Make sure the edge of the tape is parallel with the rail.

② Paint the rail by brushing along it. Paint into the angle between rail and wall first, then finish the face of the rail.

Skirting boards

Dust the top edge of the skirting and any moulding detail. Fill gaps along the top edges and in corners with mastic. Sweep or vacuum the floor. Stick masking tape to smooth floorcoverings.

If the floor is carpeted, slip strips of thin cardboard between the carpet and the bottom of the skirting. If resin from knots in the wood has discoloured the paint, sand back to bare wood and apply knotting solution. Prime and undercoat the area.

Paint the skirting board with a 50 or 75mm (2 or 3in) brush. Apply the paint in horizontal bands. Take care not to fill moulding detail with paint.

Frames and architraves

Dust the top of the architrave. Fill gaps between the architrave and wall with mastic. Stick masking tape to the walls along the edges of the architraves and over door hinges.

If you are painting only one face of the door, paint the frame as far as the edge of the door stop. Paint the face of each section of architrave next. Tuck a cardboard strip under the bottom of each side section to keep paint off carpet.

Finish by painting the edges of the architrave, brushing paint well into the angle between it and the wall.

Painting metalwork

Most of the metalwork you'll want to paint indoors will be the central heating radiators and circuit pipework, plus any other exposed plumbing pipes in rooms such as bathrooms and cloakrooms. You might also have metal windows.

you will need

→ paint *or*
→ radiator enamel
→ paint brushes
→ pipe sleeves

Before you start

Turn off each radiator and allow it to cool down before you paint it. If you paint a radiator or its pipework when it is hot, the paint will dry too quickly and its durability will be seriously affected. Avoid painting cold water pipes or metal windows on cold days, when the surface will be covered with a fine film of condensation that will prevent the new paint from sticking properly.

Pipe sleeves

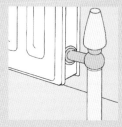

There is a neat alternative to paint for decorating the short vertical pipes that drop to the floor from most central heating radiators. It Is a white plastic pipe sleeve, which you simply cut to length with a sharp knife and slip over the pipe. It resists knocks much better than paint, and will not yellow over time as many white gloss paints do.

TIP

If you want your radiators and pipework to match the colour of your walls, use an all-surface paint (typically sold as kitchen and bathroom emulsion).

Painting a radiator

You can paint a radiator that has already been painted or primed with any one of three paint types: solvent-based gloss or eggshell paint; water-based all-surface paint; or special radiator enamel. Use the last type for a white finish that will not yellow over time.

1 Most panel radiators have vertical flutes running from top to bottom. Paint the top part of the panel first, applying the paint with horizontal brush strokes.

2 Paint the flutes next. Start at one side of the radiator and paint the recessed part first, then the adjacent raised part, using vertical brush strokes.

3 Carry on painting the rest of the flutes in the same way. Then paint the bottom part of the radiator with horizontal brush strokes, as for the top part.

4 Paint as much of the back of the radiator as you can see – and reach. You can use an angled radiator brush to reach farther than an ordinary brush.

Painting pipework

Paint your central heating and plumbing pipes with the paint you are using for your radiators. Prepare the surfaces first (see pages 62–63), then apply the paint directly over the existing paint, or the bare metal if the pipes have not been painted previously.

1 Paint pipework by brushing the paint along the pipe to begin with. Then brush round the pipe to coat it evenly before finishing off by applying light strokes along the pipe.

2 The first coat of paint will appear streaky over bare metal. Let it dry thoroughly, then apply a second coat.

Painting metal windows

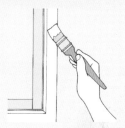

After preparing the surface (see page 63), mask off the glass with the edge of the tape about 2mm (⅛in) away from the bedding putty. Wipe the surface with a dry cloth to remove any traces of condensation from the cold metal. Then apply one or two coats of solvent-based gloss or eggshell paint.

Painting a stairwell

There are two distinct parts to the job of painting a stairwell – painting the walls and ceiling, and painting the balustrade and other woodwork. The former requires some strategically placed access equipment, the latter lots of patience.

you will need

→ ladder section
→ stepladder
→ two long scaffold boards
→ G-clamps or rope
→ paint
→ paint brushes
→ paint roller and tray
→ dust sheets

TIP

As an alternative to assembling your own access equipment, you can hire a combination ladder or a stairwell access platform from your local plant hire shop.

Providing safe access

Use a section of an extension ladder, a stepladder and a couple of long scaffold boards to create a working platform at a height that lets you reach the ceiling and the tops of the walls comfortably. Pad the top of the ladder section to protect the wall surfaces, and sandwich the two boards together with rope or G-clamps so they cannot slip or move.

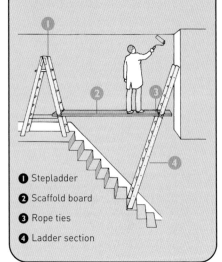

❶ Stepladder
❷ Scaffold board
❸ Rope ties
❹ Ladder section

Painting the stairwell

① After setting up your access equipment, start by painting the ceiling. Use a brush or a roller as you prefer, and steady yourself on your work platform by resting your free hand against the wall.

② Paint the walls next, starting at the top of the wall alongside which the stairs descend. Remove the access equipment as soon as you have reached a level where you can paint comfortably when standing on the stairs or landing. Finish painting the lower parts of the stairwell walls.

③ Paint any woodwork in the stairwell, including the sloping sides of the staircase (the strings) where the stairs abut a wall. If the staircase is carpeted, tuck strips of cardboard into the angle between the treads and the strings to keep paint off the carpet.

TIP

While you have the access equipment in place, clean any light fittings that are normally out of reach, and fit new light bulbs in them.

Painting the balustrade

There are no short-cuts to painting a balustrade, since each baluster has to be painted one by one. Vacuum the staircase before you start in order to minimize the amount of dust and fluff around to mar the finish.

① Paint the balusters first, using a slim paint brush. Work vertically first, then paint around each baluster to fill any details in the turning. Finish off with light vertical brush strokes. Work from both sides of the balustrade.

② Paint the newel posts at the top and bottom of the balustrade next, plus any decorative finials on the posts.

③ Finish the job by painting the handrail. Take care not to let paint build up in any of the internal angles below the handrail or where it meets the newel posts.

Stripping paint from wood

There comes a time when successive coats of paint build up to such an extent that they obscure surface detail, or stop doors and windows from closing. When you reach that point, it is time to strip everything back to bare wood and start again.

you will need

→ power sander and abrasives *or*
→ hot air gun *or*
→ chemical paint stripper
→ stripping knife
→ combination shavehook
→ protective gloves
→ metal container for stripped paint

Warning

Old paint may contain lead pigments (which are a health hazard). If you are stripping layers of paint in a pre-1960s house, be aware of this risk. You can buy test kits from paint suppliers to identify lead paints. If you suspect that they are present, use chemical strippers to remove them.

Dry sanding

You can remove old paint by sanding it, but the thicker the paint, the harder work it will be. This is because the heat created by sanding melts the paint, clogging the abrasive being used to remove it. This method is best used only on flat surfaces, where a power sander can do the work and the abrasives are disposable when clogged. A belt sander is the best tool to use for the job, and can be fitted with an integral dustbag or connected to a vacuum cleaner to keep the resulting dust under control.

Using a chemical stripper

Always use a chemical stripper if you want to varnish the bare wood; heat may char it. Various types of chemical stripper are available. Pick one that is neutralized with water rather than white spirit for ease of use. Select a thick paste type if you are stripping vertical surfaces, to minimize run-off. Always read the instructions carefully and follow any recommended safety precautions.

❶ Apply the stripper using an old paint brush, and leave it to work for the recommended time.

❷ Remove the bubbled-up paint from flat areas using a stiff stripping knife. Deposit the scrapings in a metal container for disposal later.

❸ Scrape paint from mouldings using a combination shavehook. Pull the shaped edge of the tool towards you.

❹ Apply more stripper if necessary and repeat until the wood is bare. Then wipe off and neutralize the stripper as recommended by the manufacturer.

Using a hot-air gun

Pick a hot-air gun if you have large areas to strip and you intend to repaint the stripped wood. Read the instructions before using one for the first time.

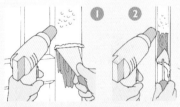

❶ Direct the hot air flow back and forth over a small area of paint until it begins to bubble and lift. Use a stripping knife to remove the paint from flat areas.

❷ Take care when stripping mouldings not to scorch the wood. Use a shavehook to strip the softened paint.

Restoring stripped woodwork

Once you have removed layers of old paint from your woodwork, you will need to carry out some repair and restoration work to get it fit for redecorating. This is especially true if you intend to stain and varnish it.

you will need

→ glasspaper
→ finishing sander
→ wood filler
→ filling knife
→ coloured wood stopper
→ knotting solution
→ small paint brush

Dip-stripped wood

You can have items such as doors and old furniture professionally stripped of old paint. This is done by immersing the item in a tank of caustic soda, which is a very effective stripping agent. When the stripped item is returned to you, scrub it thoroughly with plenty of clean water to remove all residues of the chemical from the wood before you redecorate it. Any traces of stripper will prevent the new finish from drying properly.

Sanding the surface

The very least preparation your newly stripped wood will need is sanding to leave the surface smooth.

Do this by hand using glasspaper wrapped around a sanding block for flat areas, or around a piece of dowel for mouldings.

Alternatively, use a power sander. An orbital or palm sander (1) is perfect for flat surfaces, while a detail sander (2) can reach into awkward corners.

Using wood filler

Use white wood filler to repair splits, cracks and dents in wood you intend to repaint. Take some filler on your knife and press it into the defect, then scrape off the excess and leave it to dry.

Sand the filler smooth with abrasive paper wrapped around a sanding block.

TIP

When you have finished preparing your woodwork, wipe the surface with a tack rag – a specially impregnated cloth that picks up fine sanding dust like a magnet. Alternatively, use a clean cloth slightly moistened with white spirit.

Sealing knots

Knots in wood can exude resin and discolour any subsequent decorative finish. Seal any that you expose after stripping off old paint by brushing on two coats of shellac knotting.

Removing stains

Stripping paint may reveal other blemishes, such as stains in the bare wood. If you want to stain and varnish the wood, use a proprietary two-part wood bleach to remove the discoloration. Brush one part on to the stain, then apply the second over the first after 5 to 10 minutes. When the stain has faded, neutralize the bleach with a weak solution of white vinegar in water and allow it to dry before sanding the surface smooth.

Staining and varnishing wood

Varnish enhances the appearance and colour of many woods, from humble pine to more exotic hardwoods. You can use it on its own on new and stripped wood, or experiment first with wood stains to alter the base colour of the wood.

you will need

→ varnish
→ paint brushes *or*
→ paint pads
→ lint-free cloths
→ wood stains
→ shallow containers for stains
→ fine abrasive paper
→ sanding block
→ tack rag

Applying wood stains

Use water-based wood stains rather than solvent-based ones, which tend to penetrate the wood deeply and dry quickly, making the results difficult to control. You can mix different shades of the same type if you want to create an unobtainable colour.

❶ Brush on parallel bands of stain. Don't let them overlap or you will get a deeper colour in these areas.

❷ Wipe off excess stain immediately using a clean lint-free cloth. Apply a second coat for a deeper colour.

Make a test strip

To get an idea of the depth of colour you can achieve with a wood stain, test its effect on a piece of wood similar to what you will be staining. Paint the whole strip with one coat of dye, and wipe off any excess with a clean cloth. When it is dry, apply a second coat to just two-thirds of the strip, and a third coat to the first third. This allows you to gauge the depth of colour achieved by one, two and three coats, and will allow you to select the appropriate level of colour to apply to the workpiece. Varnish the strip too if you plan to varnish the finished item.

Applying varnish

Thin the first coat of varnish by diluting it with white spirit. Apply it in adjacent, but not overlapping, bands with a clean cloth. Work parallel to the grain direction.

When the varnish has dried, sand the surface lightly with fine abrasive paper wrapped around a sanding block. Work parallel to the grain.

Apply the next coat of varnish with a brush as you would paint. Brush it along the grain first, then across the grain to get even coverage.

Finish off by drawing the brush lightly along the grain direction. Do not over-brush the finish, or you will create tiny air bubbles in the surface.

It is best to varnish doors unscrewed from their hinges and laid flat. Tackle the panel mouldings first, then the panels.

When you have completed all the panels, varnish the cross-rails, muntins and stiles to complete the job.

Stripping wallpaper

Wallpaper is a one-off decoration. Once you tire of it and want to change to a different colour scheme, it has to come off. The only exception is relief wallpaper, which is intended to be overpainted and can be refreshed with further coats of paint.

you will need

→ sponge and bucket
→ small garden spray gun
→ stripping knife
→ orbital scorer
→ steam wallpaper stripper

Before you start

Check what sort of wallcovering you are dealing with. Ordinary printed wallpaper will absorb water splashed on to it. Washables and vinyls will not. You can tell a washable from a vinyl by the fact that you can pick and lift a corner of vinyl wallpaper and peel off the plastic surface layer, leaving the backing paper on the wall. Finally, it will be obvious if you have a painted wallpaper – perhaps the most difficult of all to strip.

Stripping vinyl

As mentioned, vinyl is the easiest wallpaper to strip. Simply pick a bottom corner at a seam with your fingernail or a knife blade.

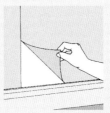

❶ Get hold of the bottom edge of the plastic layer and carefully peel it away from the backing paper, pulling it upwards in a continuous motion.

❷ When you have stripped all the vinyl, soak and scrape off the backing paper as for printed wallpaper (opposite). Do not attempt to paint or paper over the old backing paper. If you do, it will lift and bubble as you apply the new decoration, spoiling its effect.

Ordinary wallpaper

1 Soak the paper with a wet sponge or by spraying water on to it from a spray gun. Let it soak in for a few minutes.

2 Use your stripping knife to scrape the wallpaper off, section by section. Deposit the scrapings in a refuse bag so you do not tread them everywhere.

TIP

Use warm rather than cold water, and add a little bit of washing-up liquid or branded liquid wallpaper stripper.

Washable and painted wallpaper

1 Use an orbital scorer with a scrubbing motion to perforate the paper surface with hundreds of small holes. Then soak and scrape off the wallpaper.

2 Alternatively, buy or hire a steam wallpaper stripper. Fill it with water, switch it on and wait for it to boil.

3 Hold the steaming plate against the wall and allow the steam to penetrate the wallpaper. On plasterboard and old

walls with lime plaster, do not steam an area for too long, or you may soften the old plaster.

4 Use your stripping knife to remove the paper from the steamed area. At the same time, hold the steaming plate over the next area you want to strip.

5 Finish the job by washing the wall to remove any remaining nibs of paper and old wallpaper paste.

Filling cracks in walls

Once you have stripped old wallpaper, you are likely to find that the plaster behind is in less-than-perfect condition, with numerous small cracks and even small patches of plaster that are crumbling away. Fix them before you redecorate.

you will need

→ powder or ready-mixed filler
→ old paint brush
→ filling knife
→ abrasive paper and sanding block
→ small cold chisel
→ hammer
→ small garden spray gun

Filling small holes

❶ Use an old paintbrush to clean dust from the hole. Then pack in some filler with your filling knife. Leave the filler slightly proud of the surrounding surface.

❷ When the filler has set hard, use abrasive paper wrapped round a sanding block to smooth the repair.

Choosing filler

There is a huge range of fillers available, from traditional plaster types you mix with water to fast-setting ready-mixed types sold in a tub or tube. The former is by far the most economical to use if you have a lot of filling to do, but fast-setting types are worth the extra cost if you are in a hurry and want quick results. Powder fillers will keep for years if kept dry, but ready-mixed fillers have a finite shelf life and tend to separate out into liquid and sludge if allowed to stand unused for long periods.

INDOORS
filling cracks in walls

Filling cracks

Use the corner of your filling knife to rake out the crack, undercutting the edges. Then brush out the debris.

Pick up some filler on your knife and fill the crack by drawing the blade first across it, then along it. Leave the filler slightly proud of the surface.

When the filler has set hard, use abrasive paper wrapped around a sanding block to smooth it off.

Filling large holes

If you find large patches of cracked and loose plaster, chip out the area with a small cold chisel and hammer.

Brush out loose dust and debris, then wet the plaster by spraying on water from a small garden spray gun. This stops the filler drying out too quickly.

Fill the hole in layers about 12mm (½in) thick, allowing each to harden before applying the next. Use a piece of wood to level off the patch, sawing it from side to side. Sand when hard.

Repairing damaged plaster

External corners on plastered walls are the most vulnerable to accidental damage, especially in older houses where the corners would not have been reinforced. Lath-and-plaster walls in older houses are also prone to accidental damage.

you will need

→ expanded metal mesh
→ tinsnips
→ patching plaster
→ pointing trowel
→ steel plasterer's trowel
→ cold chisel and hammer
→ wooden battens
→ masonry nails
→ spirit level or straight-edge

Patching lath-and-plaster

In older houses, walls and ceilings will be finished in lath-and-plaster – a plaster layer bonded to closely-spaced wooden laths nailed to wall studs and ceiling joists. If the plaster is damaged, it can break away from the laths to leave a hole. The best way of reinforcing the repair is to fill the hole with a piece of expanded metal mesh, cut to fit.

❶ Remove debris from the area and brush away dust. Then cut a piece of mesh to size with tinsnips.

❷ Fit it in the hole and secure it with dabs of patching plaster, pressed into place with your pointing trowel.

❸ Press the first layer of plaster into the mesh with a steel plasterer's trowel. Score the surface and apply a finish coat when this layer has set.

Patching external corners

Use a cold chisel and hammer to cut away loose material from the damaged corner (cutting to the brickwork if needed).

Drive two masonry nails into a timber batten that will extend about 300mm (12in) above and below damaged area.

Position the batten against the damaged corner with its edge in line with the plaster surface on one side of the corner. Drive the nails in part-way.

Use your plasterer's trowel to fill one side of the corner, flush with the edge of the batten. Leave the plaster to set.

Prise the batten away carefully and plaster the other face of the corner, using the edge of the first patch as a guide. Take care not to damage the corner as you do this.

If the corner is likely to be damaged again by passing traffic, reinforce it before plastering it by nailing on a length of metal corner beading. Then plaster each side of the repair.

Repairing damaged plasterboard

Plasterboard is quite tough, but it is easy to knock a hole in it if you are careless in moving furniture, for example. How you go about patching it depends on how extensive the damage is.

you will need

→ glassfibre repair tape
→ plaster filler
→ filling knife
→ offcut of hardboard or MDF
→ nail and string
→ PVA wood adhesive
→ small plasterboard panel
→ plasterboard nails
→ 50 x 25mm (2 x 1in) battens
→ plasterer's trowel
→ basic toolkit

Buying plasterboard

If you need to patch a big hole in plasterboard, most DIY superstores sell small (1220 x 610mm / 4 x 2ft) sheets. Alternatively, look out for a local building site and ask the foreman if you can scrounge an offcut of board for the price of a pint. You might also find one in a skip.

Patching small holes

You can repair small holes up to about 50mm (2in) across using self-adhesive glassfibre repair tape. Stick strips across the hole, then apply filler over it.

Alternatively, cut a piece of hardboard or MDF narrow enough to fit through the hole. Make a hole in it, thread string through the hole and tie it to a nail.

Apply PVA wood adhesive to each end of the offcut, feed it into the hole and pull it against the inner face of the board until it sticks. Cut off the string and fill the hole.

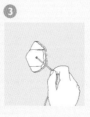

Patching large holes

Use a pencil and straight-edge to draw horizontal lines on the wall above and below the damaged area.

Use a padsaw to cut along the horizontal lines until you reach the adjacent studs. Then cut vertically alongside each stud.

Use a sharp knife to cut the board down the centres of the adjacent studs, and prise away the two strips.

Cut two pieces of batten long enough to fit between the studs, and clamp them in place so they will support the patch. Nail them to the studs at each side.

Cut a piece of plasterboard to size to fill the hole, and nail it to the studs and the two horizontal support battens.

Stick glassfibre repair tape over the joints all around the patch, then apply plaster over it with your trowel.

Fixing damaged ceilings

The commonest problem with ceilings is cracks opening up along the edges of the plasterboard sheets that form its surface. Worse still is damage resulting from a carelessly placed foot slipping off a joist in the loft and making a big hole.

you will need

→ glassfibre repair tape
→ plaster filler
→ filling knife
→ patching plaster
→ PVA wood adhesive
→ small plasterboard panel
→ plasterboard nails
→ 50 x 50mm (2 x 2in) softwood battens
→ offcut of plywood or MDF
→ timber prop
→ basic toolkit

Fixing ceiling cracks

Ceilings crack along the edges of the plasterboard sheets because the edge joints were not taped when the ceiling was first installed.

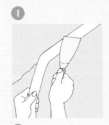

❶ Stick a length of glassfibre repair tape along each crack, pressing it into place using the edge of your filling knife.

❷ Use a filling knife to apply a band of filler over the tape, extending about 25mm (1in) on each side.

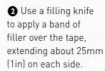

❸ Smooth off excess filler and disguise the edges of the repair by wiping over it with a damp sponge.

Repairing a bulge

If you have old lath-and-plaster ceilings, areas of plaster can become detached from their laths, resulting in an alarming downward bulge in the ceiling surface. If you are lucky, you may be able to rescue the situation by propping the bulge back up against the laths and pouring plaster over them from above. This should bond the plaster back to the laths and cure the bulge.

Repairing a hole

If your foot has gone right through a lath-and-plaster or plasterboard ceiling, cut back the damaged area to form a neat rectangular opening, as described for patching a plasterboard wall (*page 97*). Nail 50 x 50mm (2 x 2in) softwood battens between the joists to support the edges of the patch, then nail up a piece of plasterboard to fill the hole. Apply glassfibre repair tape along all four edges, then add a skim coat of plaster over the patch to conceal it.

Patching lath-and-plaster

If the plaster bulge falls away, but the old laths are still intact, cut back the plaster at the edges of the area until you have removed all loose or cracked material. Then dampen the laths with a solution of PVA wood adhesive and

water, to aid the adhesion of the new plaster. Apply a thin coat of plaster, forcing it up between the laths, and score the surface to key it for the second coat of plaster. Apply this when the first layer is hard, smoothing it off.

Putting up coving

Coving is a decorative moulding that is stuck into the wall-ceiling angle around a room to form a frame for the ceiling. It also has the advantage of concealing the cracks that often open up between the ceiling and wall.

you will need

→ coving
→ coving adhesive
→ coving mitre box
→ masonry nails
→ stepladder
→ basic toolkit

Types of coving

The most common is plasterboard coving, with a paper outer sleeve containing a plaster core. It is quite heavy. Other popular types are made from relatively expensive polyurethane foam and cheaper polystyrene. Both are much lighter than plasterboard and are easier to stick in place. The most expensive of all, and not suitable for DIY installation, is reproduction fibrous plaster coving. Each needs its own special adhesive, and heavier types may also need mechanical fixing.

Corner cuts

The most important thing to get right in putting up coving is the cutting of corner mitres. Four different cuts are involved, as shown here. Always place the ceiling edge of the coving in the base of the mitre box.

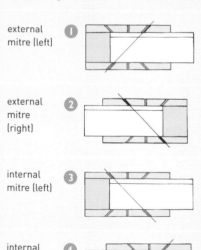

external mitre (left) ❶

external mitre (right) ❷

internal mitre (left) ❸

internal mitre (right) ❹

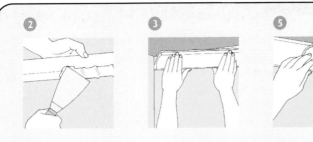

❶ Hold a length of coving in the wall-ceiling angle and mark the wall along the bottom edge. Extend this line round the room with a pencil and spirit level to form a continuous guideline.

❷ Start at an internal corner. Cut the correct mitre (see opposite) on one end, then apply adhesive along both edges of the back of the coving.

❸ Offer up the length into the room corner, aligning its lower edge with the guideline, and press it into place.

❹ Repeat the process to fit a second mitred length at the opposite end of this wall. If the two lengths overlap, cut the second to length before fitting it.

❺ If the two lengths do not meet, fit an infill piece between them. Support the coving while the adhesive dries by tapping masonry nails into the wall.

Completing the job

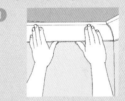

Start the second wall with a correctly mitred length. Carry on cutting and fitting sections until you return to your starting point.

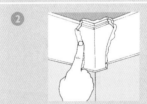

At external corners, cut the mitres as shown opposite. Use coving adhesive to fill the joints and any gaps between the coving and the wall or ceiling. Alternatively, stick on special moulded corner pieces.

Paperhanging: before you start

If you plan to wallpaper a room, there are several things you need to think about before you start. First, you have to estimate how much wallpaper you will need. Then you have to work out where best to start work. And you might need to line the walls first.

Estimating wallpaper

A standard roll of wallpaper is 10.05m (33ft) long and about 530mm (21in) wide. In a typical room, you can expect to get four full lengths out of each roll. Measure the perimeter of the room, excluding any full-height patio doors, and divide the total by the roll width to work out how many lengths you will need. Divide that figure by four to get the number of rolls required.

As an alternative to all this arithmetic, simply measure the room perimeter and ceiling height, and use the table below to see how many rolls you will need. Buy an extra roll to be on the safe side, and check that all have the same manufacturer's batch number so you can be sure the colours will match.

How to calculate the number of rolls

Distance around room	Wall height 2.3–2.4m	Wall height 2.4–2.6m	Wall height 2.6–2.7m
10m	5	5	6
12m	6	6	7
14m	7	7	8
16m	8	8	9
18m	9	9	10
20m	10	10	11

Deciding where to start

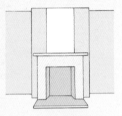

In general, it is best to start wallpapering in a corner, and to work your way around the room wall by wall until you return to your starting point.

However, if you are hanging a paper with a particularly bold pattern, it is better to try to centre the design on a main feature of the room. This may be a chimney breast if the room has one, or the wall between two windows. If the room has a door close to a corner, start papering beside the door and work around the room from there. Any pattern discontinuity can then be 'lost' in the corner behind the door.

Hanging lining paper

Lining paper is a strong, plain paper that is used (as its name implies) to line walls before a decorative wallpaper is hung. It will disguise less-than-perfect wall surfaces, giving a better finish for the patterned paper, and it also makes the final paper easier to hang if the walls have uneven porosity – as the result of some areas being freshly plastered, for example. It can be hung horizontally or vertically. Always hang it using the paste that is recommended for the decorative wallpaper, and allow it to dry out for a period of at least 12 hours before papering over it.

Follow the instructions on pages 105–121 for hanging it.

Horizontal lining

Hanging the lining paper horizontally avoids any risk of the seams coinciding with those of the decorative paper. Carry the pasted paper to the wall in concertina folds, and hang the first strip at ceiling level. Trim it into the corners at each end. Then hang subsequent strips below it, leaving a slight gap between them. Trim the final strip to width just above the skirting board. Repeat for the other walls of the room.

Vertical lining

If handling long lengths of lining paper sounds too difficult, you can always hang the paper vertically instead.

To ensure that seams do not coincide, start by hanging a half-width of paper in one corner of the room, then continue with full widths.

Sizing walls

Sizing means brushing a special sealer called size over the prepared wall surface and allowing it to dry before you start papering.

Sizing prevents wallpaper paste from drying too quickly, and allows you to slip each pasted length across the surface and into its position with ease.

Use size on bare plaster and painted and lined walls. You can sometimes use diluted wallpaper paste as size; check on the packet.

Painting lining paper

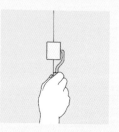

❶ Lining paper hung vertically makes the perfect base for a painted finish on less-than-perfect walls.

❷ Use a heavyweight paper (called 100 grade or 1200 grade). Butt the joints closely together, flatten them with a

seam roller and sand them lightly with fine abrasive paper when the paste has dried. This will make them virtually invisible once the paper is painted.

❸ Paint the wall with emulsion, using a large brush or roller.

Cutting and pasting wallpaper

Unless you are hanging a wallpaper with no pattern match to worry about, it is best to measure and cut each length after you have hung the previous one. In this way, you can avoid the risk of wasting paper unnecessarily.

you will need

→ wallpaper
→ wallpaper paste
→ paste bucket
→ paste brush
→ paperhanging scissors
→ pasting table

Preparing the paste

Buy enough paste to cover the number of rolls you intend to hang. Put the recommended volume of water in your paste bucket and pour in the powder while stirring vigorously with a large wooden spoon or similar implement. This will stop the paste from forming lumps. Leave it to stand for the recommended time.

Measuring and cutting

Measure the distance between the ceiling and the top of the skirting board at your chosen starting point. Add 100mm (4in) to allow for trimming at top and bottom after the length has been hung. Unroll the paper on the floor (easier than trying to do it on your pasting table), weight down the free end and measure off this distance on it. Draw a straight line across the paper and cut it with your scissors. Mark the top end (the free end of the roll) on the back of the paper.

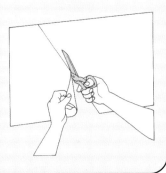

Pasting wallpaper

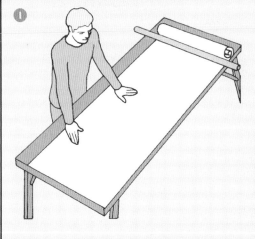

Unroll the wallpaper on your pasting table and lay a batten across the 'roll' end to keep the paper flat. Align the 'free' end of the paper with the end of the table, and the edge with the edge of the table farthest away from you.

Start brushing paste on to the paper. Work towards the far edge of the length and towards the 'free' end first.

TIP

Unless your brush has a clip that you can use to hang it inside the bucket, tie some string between the ends of the bucket handle to create a rest for the bristles.

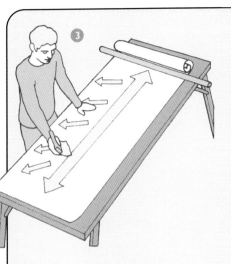

Now move the paper towards you so the unpasted edge is aligned with the near edge of the table. Brush more paste out towards this edge. This technique keeps paste off the surface of the table, and stops it marking the face of the wallpaper.

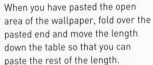

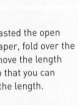

When you have pasted the open area of the wallpaper, fold over the pasted end and move the length down the table so that you can paste the rest of the length.

When you have pasted the whole length in this way, fold it into a neat concertina and leave it to soak for the time recommended on the wallpaper label – usually about 5 minutes. It will then be ready to hang.

Hanging the first length

The most important point to remember when hanging wallpaper is that corners are rarely true verticals, so they should never be used as a hanging guide. Always start papering each wall by aligning the edge of the paper to a plumbed vertical line.

Plumbing a startline

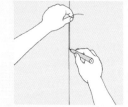

If you are starting papering in the corner of a room, measure the width of the wallpaper and subtract 25mm (1in) from this measurement. Hang your plumbline this distance from the corner and make a series of pencil marks on the wall behind the string. Join these with your pencil and straight-edge to give a true vertical line to which the first length will be hung.

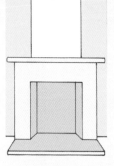

If you are hanging the first length on a prominent feature like a chimney breast or between two windows, plumb a line on the wall there.

TIP

Centre the paper on the chimney breast if possible. Before hanging the first length, check how the paper will turn into the alcove. If the turns are an awkward width, centre the plumbline and hang two lengths side by side instead.

you will need

→ plumbline
→ pencil and
   straight-edge
→ paperhanging brush

→ paperhanging
   scissors
→ seam roller

Positioning the first length

 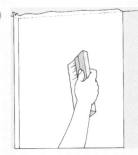

Hold the top edge of the folded paper up to the ceiling, and align its edge with your pencil guideline. Try to keep the left-hand side of the paper away from the wall as you do this. Make sure there is about 50mm (2in) of paper above the top of the wall to allow for trimming. Press the top of the length into place.

When you are happy with the alignment of the paper, brush the top part of the length into place. Then unfold the concertina to let the rest of the length hang down, and brush this into place – down the middle first, then out towards the edges and into the room corner.

Do not worry if blisters appear after you have hung the paper. They will disappear as the paste dries out and the wet paper shrinks.

Trimming the ends

 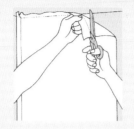

At the top of the length, crease the paper into the wall-ceiling angle with the back of the blade of your scissors. Peel the paper away from the wall and cut along the creased line.

Brush the trimmed edge back into place. Use the ends of the bristles to press the paper into the angle.

Repeat the process at the skirting board, again cutting off the waste paper and brushing the trimmed end back into place on the wall.

Check that the 25mm (1in) wide overlap on the adjacent wall is well stuck down by jabbing the bristles of your paperhanging brush into the corner. Make sure that both long edges are well stuck to the wall by running your seam roller over them. Do not do this on papers with an embossed texture: the roller will flatten it.

Paste-the-wall paper

Some wallpapers are designed to be hung dry – you paste the wall, not the wallcovering. They have a special backing that does not expand when wet, and which allows the paper to be stripped dry when you want to redecorate.

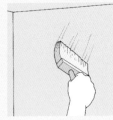

❶ Apply the paste to the wall where the first length will be hung, using a pasting brush or a paint roller. The pasted area should be slightly wider than the paper.

❷ Hang the paper direct from the roll, with a 50mm (2in) allowance for trimming at the top. Brush the paper into place from the top down, then let the rest of the roll rest on the floor while you trim the top and bottom as you would for standard wallpaper.

Ready-pasted wallpaper

Some wallpapers are still sold in ready-pasted form, with the paste coated on the back.

❶ To hang them, cut the paper to length and roll it up loosely, top end outermost.

❷ Immerse the roll in a plastic trough of cold water positioned next to the skirting board.

❸ After allowing it to soak for the recommended time, draw the top of the length upwards and position it on the wall as for standard wallpaper.

❹ The excess water will run back into the trough as you draw the paper out. Take care not to step in the trough as you hang the paper.

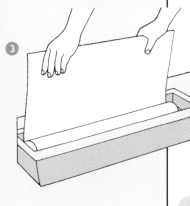

Papering around corners

Once the first length is in place, you repeat the process to hang adjacent lengths along the wall, butting their edges together and rolling the seams flat for almost invisible joins. But eventually you will come to the next corner...

Turning an internal corner

When you have hung the last full width on the wall you are papering, measure the distance from its edge to the corner at the top, centre and bottom of the wall and add 25mm (1in) to the largest measurement. Cut a strip of paper to this width. Save the offcut.

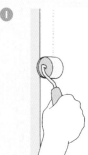

TIP

If you are hanging a washable or vinyl wallpaper, the paste will not stick the overlap down. You need to use special vinyl overlap adhesive, which is sold in tubes. Squeeze a thin bead of it on to the face of the turned strip and press the overlapping piece firmly into place. Wipe away any excess adhesive that oozes out using a damp cloth.

Paste and hang the strip, butting its edge against the last full width hung. Brush it well into the corner.

Use your seam roller to ensure that the narrow turned strip is firmly stuck to the wall. If creases form in the paper, tear it carefully and overlap the pieces.

The golden rule

Because corners are rarely truly vertical, never try to turn more than about 50mm (2in) of paper on to the next wall. The turned edge will not be vertical, and if you use it as a guide for hanging the full widths on the next wall, they will all run out of true – with potentially disastrous results if there is a horizontal motif in the design.

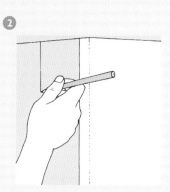

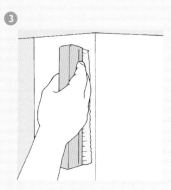

Measure the width of the offcut and mark the wall at that distance from the corner of the room. Plumb a guide line through the mark.

Paste and hang the offcut to the guideline. Brush its scissor-cut edge firmly into the corner, overlapping the strip turned from the previous wall. Match the pattern as best you can.

TIP

Because of the overlap, you will not be able to get an exact pattern match in the corner. Obtain the best match you can; the eye will not notice the discrepancy.

External corners

 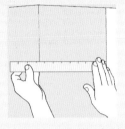

 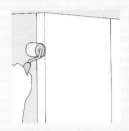

When you have hung the last full length before the corner, measure the distance to the corner at the top, centre and bottom of the wall as for internal corners. Add 25mm (1in) to the largest measurement. Cut a strip to this width and save the offcut.

Paste the strip and hang it, butting one edge against that of the last full width and taking the 25mm (1in) wide strip onto the adjacent wall. Make sure the strip is firmly stuck down by running a seam roller over it.

 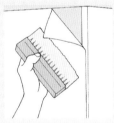

Measure the width of the offcut, add 15mm (⅝in) and plumb a line on the next wall this distance from the corner. Paste and hang the offcut to this line, sticking its scissor-cut edge over the turned strip and matching the pattern as well as you can. Use overlap adhesive for washables and vinyls (see TIP on *page 112*).

Double corners

You may be faced with papering around three corners close together – for example, where pipework is boxed in at the corner of a room. Never try to take paper around more than one corner. The best solution is to paper into the first internal corner, with an overlap on to the boxing. Then paper into the second internal corner from the next wall, again with an overlap. Finally, cut a strip wide enough to paper both faces of the boxing and hang this so it overlaps the narrow strips in each internal corner. Get the best pattern match you can.

Papering around doors and windows

The next obstacles you will encounter as you paper your way around the room are door and window openings. Each requires a different paperhanging technique to guarantee a neat fit at the obstacle.

Papering around a door

Hang a full length of paper so it laps over the architrave. Press the paper over the top corner to mark it, then make a cut upwards at 45° to the mark.

Crease the tongues of paper into the angles between wall and architrave with scissors, then trim each off and brush the paper back into the angles.

Cut and paste a short length of paper to fit above the door, and brush it into place. Trim it at the ceiling and along the top of the architrave.

Hang the next full strip at the other side of the door and deal with the overlap on to the architrave as in steps 1 and 2. Plumb a guideline for this length, to ensure that it is truly vertical.

Papering window recesses

①

When you reach the window, hang a full length so it overlaps the recess. Brush the paper on to the face wall above and below the recess.

②

Make horizontal release cuts level with the top of the recess and at sill level. This will allow the tongue of paper to fold back on to the side of the recess.

③

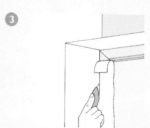

Brush the flap into the angle and trim off the excess. If using a knife, keep the blade at a shallow angle. If the paper is too narrow to reach the frame, fill the gap with a narrow strip.

TIP

This cutting and fitting procedure is quite fiddly, and the edges of the paper may start to dry out as you work. Bring a mug of paste and a small paint brush to the window sill so you can repaste any dry edges and stick them down.

④

Hang short lengths above and below the window. Above the window, brush the paper into the angle where it meets the frame, and trim off the excess.

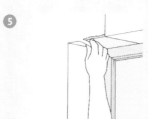

⑤

Return to the edge of the first length above the recess. If you are hanging a printed or washable wallpaper, carefully tear off a narrow strip along its lower edge. Cut and fit a patch to cover the underside of the recess. Brush its front edge onto the wall above the recess.

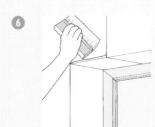

⑥

Then cover the edge of the patch with the edge of the paper torn in step 5, and brush it down to leave an almost invisible join. If hanging a vinyl, overlap the layers of paper and cut through them with a sharp knife to leave a neat butt joint.

Beyond the window

Hang a full length of paper at the other side of the recess to meet the pieces you hung above and below it in step 4. Check that this length is vertical using a plumbline. If it is not, let it overlap the paper edge above the recess, where it will be less noticeable than below it.

❶ Trim the overlap into the recess as in steps 1 to 3. If it does not reach the window frame, hang a narrow strip of paper to cover the side of the recess.

❷ Patch the top corner of the recess as in steps 5 and 6.

Papering: the fiddly bits

There are two final obstacles you are likely to come up against when papering a room. The first are light switches and socket outlets, and the second are radiators. Here's how to get around both neatly.

Papering around switches

Paper over each switch or socket outlet. Then press the paper against its faceplate to indent it at each corner.

Pierce the paper over the centre of the faceplate and make a 45° cut out to each corner to create four flaps.

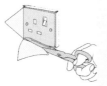

Press each flap into the angle between the wall and faceplate, and trim it to leave a 3mm (⅛in) overlap.

Turn the power off at the mains and loosen the faceplate screws. Brush the flaps behind the faceplate, then tighten the screws to trap them neatly.

Papering around a radiator

When you reach a radiator, measure the distance between the top of the radiator and the top of the wall bracket behind it.

Stick masking tape to the radiator in line with the bracket position. Mark on it the distance you measured in step 1. Repeat for the other bracket.

Hang the next length of paper so it falls over the radiator, and slit it up from its bottom edge as far as the mark on the masking tape.

Alternative

An alternative to the above technique is simply to trim each length of paper short and tuck about 150mm (6in) down behind the radiator. What the eye doesn't see...

Tuck the two strips of paper down behind the radiator using a slimline radiator roller. Hang more lengths behind the radiator, and repeat the slitting technique when you reach the other bracket. Trim off the excess at the bottom of each strip and press it into place above the skirting board. Apply a little extra paste if the ends have dried out. Then carry on hanging full lengths on the wall beyond the radiator.

Papering ceilings and stairwells

Once you have got the hang of hanging paper, there are two more challenges you might fancy tackling. The first is to paper a ceiling – actually easier than it looks – and the second is to paper a stairwell.

Papering a ceiling

There are three things you need to make papering a ceiling a manageable undertaking. The first is to have decent access equipment – ideally a low-level platform that spans the full width of the room. The second is to take down any light fittings (see page 55). The third is to have a helper.

The simplest access set-up is a pair of stepladders bridged by a trestle, or by a pair of scaffold boards sandwiched together and clamped or tied to the steps. Hire the equipment if you do not own it.

❶ Pin a stringline across the ceiling, 25mm (1in) less than the roll width away from the side wall.

❷ Paste and fold the paper into a concertina and get your helper to hold it behind you while you position the end of the length in the wall-ceiling angle.

❸ Brush the length into place while your partner frees successive folds of the concertina. Then trim the ends and the long side edge into the wall-ceiling angle. Repeat for subsequent lengths.

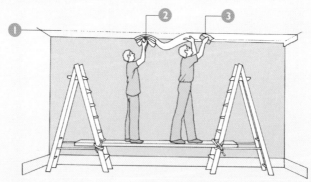

Papering a stairwell

This is the ultimate paperhanging challenge, because of the long lengths of paper needed on the side wall – often nearly half a roll's worth. It's another job where you need the right access equipment and preferably a second pair of hands.

❶ Start work on the long side wall, hanging the longest length first. Set up an access platform, as shown, using a ladder section and two scaffold boards tied or clamped in place. Alternatively, hire a staircase access tower.

❷ Work up the stairs length by length. Hang the top part of each length from the platform while your helper holds the rest of the concertina of paper below. Then brush the lower part into place and trim it where it meets the angled side of the staircase. When you reach the landing, continue hanging paper as for a normal room. In the hall, hang lengths by working away from the edge of the first long length hung.

❸ Finish off by papering the head wall above the flight. Position the top of each length working from the ladder, then set it aside and smooth the rest of the length into place. Set up a low-level work platform, as shown, to do this.

Always tie the scaffold boards to the ladder and steps so that they cannot move as you walk on them.

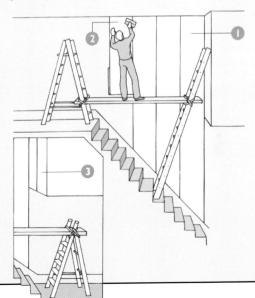

Tiling walls: where to start

Tiling is easy: you just have to coat the walls with adhesive, press the tiles into place and fill the gaps between them. The tricky part is the setting out. Because tiles are relatively small, they need to be centred on the wall if they are to look right.

you will need

→ tiles
→ tile spacers
→ timber straight-edge
→ pencil
→ 50 x 19mm (2 x ¾in) softwood battens
→ masonry nails
→ basic toolkit

TIP

You should never trust a skirting board to be a truly horizontal guide for your tiling; doing so can force all the tiles out of alignment, with potentially disastrous results. Instead a horizontal guide batten is always used to support the lowest row of whole tiles on a wall.

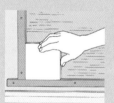

TIP

Tile spacers come in a range of sizes. Use the smallest spacers with 100 or 150mm (4 or 6in) square tiles, and wider spacers with larger square or rectangular tiles. Buy plenty – they are very cheap, and you do not want to run out half-way through the job.

Making a tile gauge

To help you set out your tiles, make a simple device called a gauge stick. Lay out a row of the tiles you will be using, with spacers between them, and place a timber straight-edge alongside.

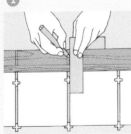

Mark the positions of the tiles and gaps on the gauge, and number the gaps from one end for easy reference. If you are using rectangular tiles, mark out a second rod to match the longer edges of the tiles.

Setting a half-tiled wall

1 One of the simplest tiling projects is to half-tile an unobstructed wall. This will have a row of whole tiles at the top, and probably a row of cut tiles at skirting board level.

2 Decide on the height of the tiled area and make a light pencil mark on the wall at that point.

3 Hold your gauge stick vertically so that one of the marks is aligned with the mark on the wall and the end is as close as possible to the skirting. If the gap between the end of the stick and the skirting is less than a third of a tile width, move the wall mark up a little. Mark the wall level with the bottom of the gauge stick.

Centring the rows

The next job is to ensure that you have cut tiles of equal width at each end of the horizontal rows.

This makes the tiled area look symmetrical – always the aim of the professional tiler.

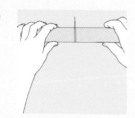

Mark the centre point of the wall and hold your tile gauge up to it so a tile mark coincides with the wall mark.

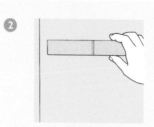

Look at the end of the gauge stick to see how wide the cut pieces of tile will be. If they will be less than a third of a tile wide, it is best to reposition the centre point.

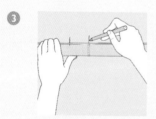

Move the gauge stick along by half a tile width and make a new mark on the wall. This will represent the new centre line of the tiling.

Align a tile mark on the gauge rod with this new mark, and repeat step 2 to check the new width of the cut tile at the end of the row. Make a mark here and draw a vertical line down the wall at this point.

Fixing the guide battens

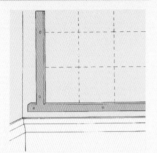

❶ You now have one mark on the wall to indicate the level of the bottom edge of the lowest row of whole tiles, and a guide line at one side to show where the outer edge of the last column of whole tiles will go.

❷ Nail a horizontal batten to the wall in line with the first, and a vertical batten in line with the second. Part-drive the nails so you can pull them out easily later.

TIP

Use masonry nails to fix the battens to a solid wall. They should penetrate the wall by about 25mm (1in) and project from the battens by 12mm (½in) or so. Drill pilot holes in the battens first so the nails do not split them. Use oval wire nails to fix the battens to a hollow partition wall.

Setting out whole walls

Tiling a whole wall will generally involve coping with obstacles such as window and door openings.

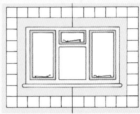

Use your gauge stick to see how the tiles will fit best. Ideally the tiling should be centred on the obstacle – a window, for example.

If the obstacle is offset – a door in a corner, for example – it is best to centre the tiles on the wall beside it.

Tiling basics

Once you have completed the setting out of the tiles and nailed up your guide battens, you are ready to start tiling for real. The battens will ensure that the tile rows and columns are perfectly aligned and will look really professional.

you will need

→ tiles
→ tile spacers
→ tile adhesive
→ adhesive spreader
→ tile cutting jig

Estimating quantities of tiles

❶ Work out how many tiles you will need to tile an area by counting the number of tiles in each horizontal row (including cut tiles), and the number of rows including the row of cut tiles at skirting board level.

❷ Multiply the two figures together, and add an extra 5 per cent to allow for any mistakes you make when cutting tiles.

Adhesive

❶ Tile adhesive comes ready-mixed in tubs, usually with a free plastic notched adhesive spreader included.

❷ There will be a coverage figure given on the tub.

❸ Measure the height and width of the area you are tiling, multiply the two figures together to get the area, and use this figure to work out how much adhesive you will need.

Placing the first tiles

Scoop some adhesive out of the tub and spread it in bands on the wall. Rest the bottom edge of the first tile on the horizontal batten and press it into position. Make sure it is also touching the vertical batten.

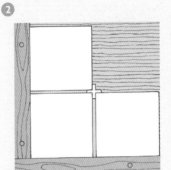

Add the tile next to it and the tile above it. Then press a tile spacer into the intersection between the tiles.

TIP

Work on no more than 1sq m (1sq yd) at a time, otherwise the adhesive will begin to go off before you finish positioning all the tiles.

TIP

Hold the spreader at an angle of 45° to the wall; this will create ridges of even height that will be compressed into a bed of adhesive of consistent thickness as you press the tiles into place.

Completing the field

❶ Continue placing whole tiles in rows and columns until you have filled the entire area. Carefully prise off the vertical guide batten so you can finish off by fitting the cut edge tiles.

❷ Wipe any smears of adhesive off the tiles as you work, and check that all the tile spacers are pressed well into the adhesive so the grouting will hide them later on.

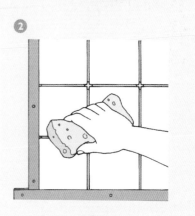

Cutting tiles

You can cut tiles using a pencil-style cutter, but life will be much easier and your cuts more accurate if you use a tile-cutting jig. This holds the tile in position, scores it precisely and snaps the tile cleanly along the cutting line. Read the instructions supplied with the jig and practise a couple of cuts first to get the hang of how it works.

❶ Cutting gauge

❷ Tile

❸ Guide base

❹ Sliding cutter

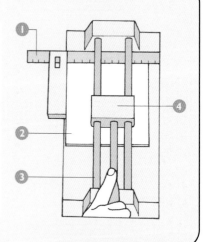

Fitting the edge tiles

①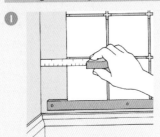

At each side of the area, measure the width of the space to be filled and subtract twice the thickness of the spacers you are using to obtain the tile width. Cut the tile to size and spread some adhesive on the back.

②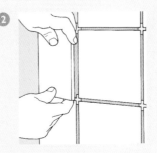

Press the cut piece into place at the edge of the area, adding spacers to keep it in line with its neighbours. Repeat to fill in all the cut edge tiles.

③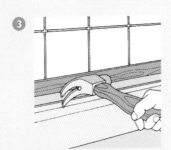

When the adhesive has set, carefully prise off the horizontal guide batten by pulling out the partly-driven nails used to secure it.

④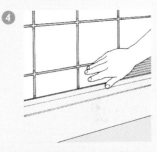

Cut and place the pieces of cut tile to fit between the lowest row of whole tiles and the skirting board.

Tiling around corners and windows

Most tiling projects will involve more than half-tiling a single wall. This means mastering the techniques for tiling internal and external corners, and for fitting tiles around window recesses.

Tiling internal corners

①

Tile the first wall and fit cut pieces at each end. Then whole-tile the adjacent wall and cut pieces to fit. Use spacers to ensure even gaps between tiles.

②

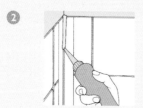

Fill the internal corner joint with non-setting mastic. Apply masking tape at each side of the joint, pipe in the mastic and smooth it off. Peel off the tape immediately to leave perfect edges.

Tiling external corners

①

If the tiles have glazed edges, simply overlap corners. Tile one wall first, flush with the corner. Then tile the other wall, aligning the tile edges.

②

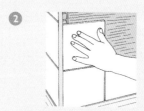

For tiles without glazed edges, use plastic corner trim. Tile one wall as in step 1, then apply adhesive to the other wall and bed in the flange of the strip. Butt tiles on the next wall up to the trim.

Tiling around window recesses

Place whole tiles up to the recess. Then cut tiles to fit between the last whole row below the recess and its front edge.

Use a tile saw (*see page 132*) to cut L-shaped pieces to fit at the bottom corners of the recess. Fit them in place.

To tile within the recess, bed plastic corner trim in adhesive along the front and sides of the recess, mitring the corners for a neat finish.

Place whole tiles on the sill and up the sides of the recess, butting them up against the plastic trim. Then fit cut pieces into the corners at each side.

Complete the tiling by fitting cut pieces of tile between the whole tiles and the window frame.

 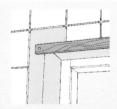

If you plan to tile the whole window wall, nail a batten above the window to support the row of tiles above it. Then fit the cut tiles round the edges.

Tiling: the fiddly bits

Apart from taking tiles around corners, you are likely to come across a variety of other challenges, such as cutting curved shapes to fit around washbasins, and fitting tiles around pipes. Then there are all the joints between the tiles to fill...

you will need

→ paper or card for templates
→ pencil
→ tile saw
→ tile nibblers
→ grout
→ grout spreader
→ grout shaper
→ sponge and duster

Cutting curves

❶ Make a paper or card template of the shape you need to copy. The template should be the same size as the tile you are using. Mark the shape on the tile.

❷ Clamp the tile in the jaws of your workbench and use a tile saw to cut slowly and carefully along the line.

Tiling around pipes

❶

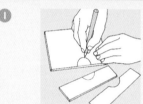

Cut a tile in two to fit it around a pipe. Use two paper or card templates to mark the cut-outs on each piece of tile.

❷

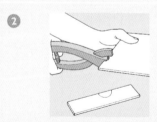

Use tile nibblers to bite away the waste areas bit by bit. Butt the two pieces of tile together around the pipe.

Grouting tiles

 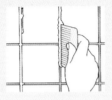

Scoop some grout with your spreader and fill the vertical joints first. Press the grout well in and scrape off any excess.

 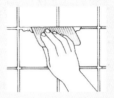

Repeat the process to fill the horizontal joints. Prise out any spacers you find that are standing proud of the tile surface.

 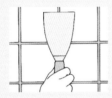

Run a stiff scraper over all the joint lines to remove any grout that's proud of the tile surface before it has a chance to set hard.

 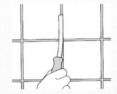

Use a plastic grout shaper to give all the grout lines a neat concave finish. Alternatively, use a piece of wooden dowel – but never a fingertip!

Use a damp sponge to wipe any remaining grout from the surface of the tiles. Rinse the sponge in clean water from time to time as you work.

Allow the grout to set hard – check the time given on the container. Then polish the haze off the surface of the tiles with a clean, dry duster.

Tiling: finishing touches

When you've finished tiling and grouting, there are a couple of jobs you might still want to do. And if you've got some existing tiling that's in need of a spruce-up, here are some tips to make it look as good as new.

Sealing joints

Grout is too rigid to make a good waterproof joint where tiling meets surfaces such as basins, baths and sinks. The best way of sealing these joints is with a bead of non-setting silicone mastic.

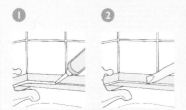

❶ Apply strips of masking tape to each surface, about 3mm (⅛in) away from the internal angle. Then apply a bead of mastic along the joint.

❷ Smooth out any lumps and bumps by drawing a plastic shaping tool or a moistened finger along the bead. Then peel off the masking tape.

Mounting accessories

You may want to fix wall-mounted accessories to your newly-tiled walls. This will involve drilling holes in the tiles – a potentially tricky job. You can buy a special ceramic tile bit for your power drill, or else use a new sharp masonry drill bit.

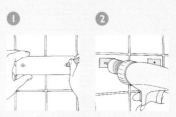

❶ Mark the positions of the screw holes through the accessory with a felt-tip pen or a Chinagraph pencil.

❷ Stick masking tape over each mark to stop the drill bit from skidding, and drill the holes. Insert wall plugs and screw on the fitting.

Restoring grotty grout

If existing tiles are sound, but the grout is badly discoloured, there are several methods you can use to clean it up.

❶ Brush a solution of household bleach diluted 1:5 with water on to the grout lines and leave it for 24 hours. Then wash the surface with clean water.

❷ Use a household steam cleaner to blast the dirt out of the grout lines. Fit the finest nozzle available.

❸ If the grout surface is smooth, but soiled, use a grout pen to restore its colour. This resembles a felt-tip pen; just draw it along all the grout lines.

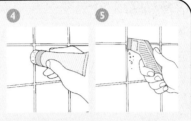

❹ If the grout surface is rough, use a grout sponge (which resembles a tube of travel shoe polish) to whiten the lines. Alternatively, brush on special grout paint with the brush supplied.

❺ If the grout is beyond saving, dig it out with a toothed tool called a grout rake. Draw it along the lines to remove the old grout, then regrout the area.

Replacing a damaged tile

If you come across individual tiles that have been cracked by an accidental impact, or have a hole from a wall-mounted fixing you have subsequently removed, it is possible to hack the tile out and replace it. Use a matching spare tile if you have any left over from the original job; otherwise buy a feature tile and fit that instead.

❶ Rake out the grout around the edges of the damaged tile. Then use a small cold chisel and a hammer to chip out the tile piece by piece, working from the centre outwards. Take care not to damage adjacent tiles.

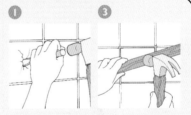

❷ Scrape out as much of the old dried adhesive as you can. Then spread tile adhesive on the back of the new tile. You can buy a tube for small repairs.

❸ Press the new tile into place, with an even gap all round. Then bed it flush with its neighbours using a timber offcut and gently tap with a hammer. Grout round it to complete.

Fixing door problems

Doors get a lot of wear and tear – they are opened, slammed and bumped into several times a day. So it is small wonder that they develop various minor niggles as time goes by. Here's how to fix the most common problems.

Doors that bind

There are two common causes of doors 'binding' or rubbing against the door frame as they close. The first is loose hinge screws, the second a build-up of too much paint on the closing edge of the door.

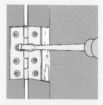

❶ Check whether the screws in the top hinge have worked loose, allowing the door to drop towards the frame. If they have, try tightening them. Replace the old screws with longer ones if the old ones will not grip.

❷ If there is a build-up of paint on the door edge, use a Surform planer file to remove the paint. Sand the door edge smooth and repaint it.

Doors that scuff

If you've recently had new carpet fitted, you may find that the door scuffs it. The solution is to trim a little off the bottom of the door. You may also need to do this if you are putting down a laminate or ceramic floor.

❶ Take the door off its hinges and lay it on your workbench. Mark a cutting line across it and saw along the line, using a hand saw or circular saw. Sand the door bottom smooth.

❷ Prop the shortened door back in position on two wedges, and reattach the hinges to the frame.

Doors that won't shut

If a door is difficult to close and tends to spring open, the problem usually lies with the hinge screws or with the hinges themselves.

❶ Check that the heads of the hinge screws fit flush in their recesses. If the heads are too big or the screws have been driven in at an angle, they will prevent the hinge from closing. Fit screws with smaller heads and make sure they are driven in straight. Drill new holes for the screws if necessary.

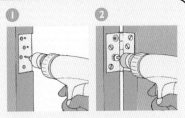

❷ An alternative is to open up the countersunk holes in the hinge flaps. Remove the screws and use a countersink bit in your power drill to enlarge them, then replace the screws.

❸ If the hinge recesses have been cut too deep, take out the screws and slip a piece of thin cardboard into the recess. Replace the screws.

Doors that rattle

If your door rattles when it is closed or the latch does not engage properly, you need to reposition the metal keeper on the door frame. Move the keeper inwards to stop rattles, and up or down to make the latch engage.

❶ Unscrew the keeper from the door frame. To reposition it nearer the door stop, use a chisel and hammer to cut away the edge of the recess.

❷ Offer up the keeper against the new edge and use a bradawl to mark the new screw holes. Replace the keeper and test the operation of the door.

❸ To move the keeper up or down, remove it and use a chisel to cut away the top or bottom of the recess. You will probably also have to enlarge the deeper hole in the frame. Then replace the keeper and test the door.

Fitting new door handles

When you are redecorating, the finishing touches can make or break the job. Old door handles may spoil the look of a freshly painted door, but fitting new ones is a straightforward job.

you will need

→ new door handle
  plus
→ new spindle and fixing screws
→ filler
→ filling knife
→ sponge sanding block
→ basic tool kit
→ paint
→ paint brush

Choosing new handles

Door handles come in a huge range of materials and styles. In general, you can fit any type you choose to a door.

Handles are usually sold in pairs, complete with a square metal spindle that connects the two handles, and with fixing screws to match the handle finish.

There are two situations where you need to match the handle type to what is there.

❶ Doors with a key-operated lock (usually on a back door).

❷ Bathroom and toilet doors with a privacy lock.

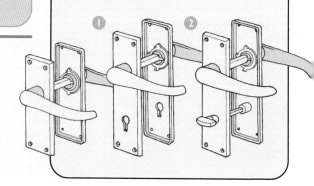

Removing the old handles

Most handles are screwed to the door, but some are secured to the spindle with a grub screw. Undo to release the handle.

Where the handle has a separate baseplate, unscrew this from the door. Repeat the process on the other face of the door to replace both handles.

Preparing the door

It is unlikely that the screw positions on the new handle will match those you have removed. Fill the old screw holes with quick-drying filler.

Sand the filled areas smooth with a sanding block. Use this to rub down ('key') the surface of the rest of the door, ready for repainting. Give the door one or two coats of paint.

Fitting the new handle

 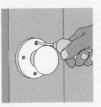

Fit the new spindle into the latch with the new handle. Mark the positions of the screws on the door using a bradawl.

Lift the handle off and enlarge the marked screw holes with the bradawl. Use a twist drill bit and power drill to make pilot holes in a hardwood door.

 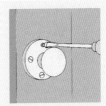

Fit the handle back on its spindle, align it with the pilot holes and screw it on. Repeat the process to fit the second handle to the other face of the door.

Replacing old hinges

If your door has old hinges that are looking scruffy and are covered with coats of old paint, replacing them with new ones will give a new or repainted door a smart fresh look. It may also eliminate some common door problems.

you will need

→ new hinges
→ new fixing screws
→ door wedges
→ 8mm (⅜in) dowel drill bit
→ 8mm (⅜in) hardwood dowels
→ PVA wood adhesive

Choosing new hinges

Most room doors are hung on two steel hinges, with leaves (the two flat parts) measuring 75 x 20 or 25mm (3 x ¾ or 1in).

Try to choose new hinges with leaves the same size as those you are replacing. The best hinges are cast from solid metal (steel or brass), and have small washers fitted around the pin between the interlocking tongues of each leaf. Cheaper hinges without washers wear more quickly.

Removing the old hinges

If the hinges have been painted over, use a sharp trimming knife to cut through the paint around all three sides of each hinge recess. This will minimize paintwork damage when you lever out the old hinge.

Scrape paint from the slots in the old screws, then undo them. If they will not move, hold the screwdriver in the slot and strike its handle sharply with a hammer.

Fitting the new latch

TIP

If the new spindle is too long, clamp it in your workbench and cut it down to size with your junior hacksaw.

Fit the new latch at the same level as the one on the old door so you will not have to reposition the keeper on the door frame. Use the old door as a template for positioning the new latch.

Hold the latch against the door face and draw around it. Then use a flat wood bit to drill a hole of the right diameter (usually 22mm / 7/8in) in the door edge. Tape on the bit shows the hole depth.

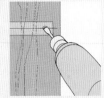

Hold the latch against the face of the door again and mark the spindle position on the door. Drill a 10mm (3/8in) diameter hole right through the door at this point.

Push the latch into the hole and use a sharp knife to mark around its faceplate on the door edge. Pull the latch out by gripping its tongue with pliers.

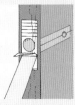

Use a chisel and hammer to chop out the recess for the faceplate. Take care not to overshoot and damage the door.

Push the latch back in the hole to test its fit. Insert the spindle and check it turns freely. Make pilot holes and screw the faceplate to the door, then the handles.

Replacing architraves

Architraves are the decorative timber mouldings that frame a door opening and hide the joint between the wall plaster and the door frame. Replacing old ones is the perfect accompaniment for a new room door.

you will need

→ architrave moulding
→ scrap wood
→ 38mm (1½in) oval wire nails
→ 25mm (1in) panel pins
→ PVA wood adhesive
→ glasspaper
→ basic toolkit

Mitre saw jig

You need to cut perfect 45° mitres at the top corners of the architrave. While you can do this reasonably accurately using a mitre box and a tenon saw, you will get far better results by using an inexpensive mitre saw jig. This allows you to set the cutting angle precisely, and also clamps the wood in place while you cut it.

Removing the old architrave

Insert a wide chisel into the gap between the architrave and the wall. Prise it away. Use some scrap wood between the chisel and wall to protect the plaster.

Repeat the process to prise off the side sections. If there is no gap down the wall edge, insert the chisel between architrave and frame, this time using scrap wood to protect the door. Remove any old nails left in the frame.

Fitting the new architrave

Hold a moulding against the frame and mark the position of the inner corner. Use the old architrave as a guide.

 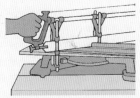

Set your mitre saw jig to 45° and cut the moulding at the mark. Check that you are sawing in the right direction.

Tap wire nails into the mouldings at 450mm (18in) intervals, align them with the frame and drive in the nails. Then punch in and fill the nail heads.

 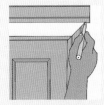

Hold a short piece of moulding upside down on top of the two side pieces and mark the positions of the two outer corners. Cut them in your mitre jig.

Put some wood glue on each end of the top section and fit it in place, Use two nails to secure it to the door frame. Wipe away any excess adhesive.

To prevent the mitre joints from opening up, drive panel pins into each joint. Sand the architrave, ready for priming and painting.

Hanging a new front door

This job is similar in principle to replacing a room door, but with one big difference: you have to finish the job by bedtime, so you can lock up for the night and know that your house is secure. Consequently, this needs some careful planning.

you will need

→ door
→ hinges and screws
→ new cylinder lock
→ new mortise lock
→ new letterbox flap
→ new door number
→ new doorknob and knocker (optional)
→ door wedges
→ basic toolkit

Choosing a new door

Exterior doors come in a range of standard sizes, the most common being 2030 x 810mm (6ft 8in x 2ft 8in). All are 45mm (1¾ in) thick. Measure your old door and try to buy one the same size. If you cannot, buy the next size up and ask your supplier to saw and plane it to size for you.

Planning the job

Because of the need to get the new door fitted in a day, some careful job planning is essential. The secret is to do as much preliminary work on your new door as possible before the day when you want to hang it. Then there will be little risk of not finishing the job on time.

❶ Use the old door as a template to position the hinges and locks in the same place on the new door. This will avoid having to make time-consuming alterations to the door frame to fit hinges and lock keepers.

❷ Buy new locks unless the old ones are in good condition and meet the security requirements of your house insurance company. An upgrade is probably well worth considering.

❸ Install door furniture such as letterbox flap, knobs, knocker and numbers in advance. Think about adding extra security features such as hinge bolts, door chain and peephole too.

❹ Finally, paint or varnish the door.

Preparing the new door

This a summary of the main stages involved in getting your new front door ready for hanging.

See pages 141 for plugging holes, 140 for door hinges, 148–149 for cylinder locks, 154–155 for mortise locks, 150–151 for door furniture

   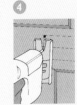

① Choose new door hinges to match the size of the existing ones. Mark and chisel out the hinge positions to match those on the existing door, and fit the hinges in place.

② Install the new cylinder lock on the door so you will be able to secure it at the end of the day.

③ Install the new mortise lock and its escutcheon plate. If the existing door does not have one, you will have to fit its keeper to the door frame once the door has been hung.

④ Fit door furniture such as a letterbox flap and a door knocker. The former needs a rectangular hole cut in the door, the latter just a bolt hole.

Hanging the door

With all the preparation done, you are ready for the big day. Unscrew the old door, plug the screw holes in the frame (*see page 139*) and screw the new hinges into the existing recesses.

Replace the existing keeper for the cylinder lock with the new one, so you can lock the door securely. You may have to make some minor adjustments to the recess in the door frame to fit it.

Fitting a cylinder lock

A cylinder lock that can be deadlocked from inside and outside the house is the bare minimum a front door should have for good security. Because the lock can be opened from inside at the turn of a knob, it also provides daytime convenience.

you will need

→ cylinder lock
→ 32mm (1¼in) flat wood bit
→ basic toolkit

Choosing a cylinder lock

Any cylinder lock should either deadlock (be resistant to forcing) automatically as the door shuts, or should be capable of being deadlocked from either side with a key once the door has been closed.

① Deadlock **③** Cylinder

② Keeper

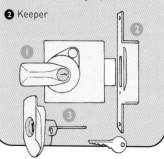

Drilling the cylinder hole

①

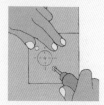

Decide at what level on the door you want to fit the lock. Use the paper template supplied with the lock to mark the centre of the cylinder hole on the door.

②

Use a 32mm (1¼in) flat wood bit in your drill to make the hole for the cylinder. When the point of the bit emerges, turn the door over and complete the hole from the other side to avoid splintering the door face as the bit emerges.

Fitting the lock

 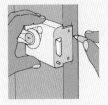

Hold the lock body in position and draw around its flange on the door edge. Cut along the lines with a trimming knife.

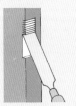
Chisel out the recess in the door edge, taking care not to overshoot and damage the door. Test the lock's fit.

Insert the cylinder in its hole and fit the lock body over the end of the connecting bar to see if it is too long. If it is, cut the bar to length with a junior hacksaw.

Screw the lock mounting plate to the inner face of the door. Then insert the cylinder in its hole and screw it through the holes in the mounting plate.

 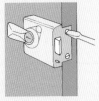 

Fit the lock body on to the lugs on the mounting plate. Then drill pilot holes into the door edge for its fixing screws, and screw the lock body to the door.

Close the door and mark the position of the keeper on the door frame. Chisel out recesses for the keeper's faceplate and the lock bolt, and screw it into place.

Fitting door furniture

Door furniture is a quaint term for all the bits of hardware that turn a front door into an advertisement for an ironmonger's store. It includes letterbox flaps, knobs, knockers, house numbers and little escutcheon plates to cover the keyhole.

Knobs and knockers

An ornamental door knob gives you something to use to pull the door closed as you go out. A knocker fitted higher up on the door adds to its style, and is a low-tech alternative to a door bell. Both are very simple to fit, usually requiring just a single hole drilled through the door. You may also need to screw on a separate strike plate for the knocker.

❶ If the fixing bolt has a screw head, form a counterbore for it on the inside of the door.

❷ If the fixing is a stud and nut, cut off the excess from the stud with a hacksaw.

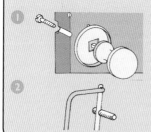

Pulls and escutcheons

Knobs do not suit flush doors. Instead, you can fit a cylinder pull around the rim of a cylinder lock. You have to remove the cylinder from the lock to fit it.

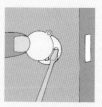

Fit an escutcheon with a swing-aside cover plate on the outside of the door to prevent draughts from blowing through the keyhole. Add a plain one with no cover on the inside.

Fitting a letterbox flap

 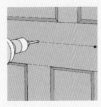

Centre the flap on the centre rail if the door has one. Mark the positions of the fixing studs and drill their holes.

Draw a rectangle on the door face. Make sure there is at least 15mm (⅝in) of solid wood between it and the stud holes.

 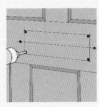

Drill a hole inside each corner of the rectangle, large enough to admit the blade of your jigsaw – about 10mm (⅜in) will be ideal.

Insert the jigsaw blade in one hole, start cutting along the first side of the rectangle and work your way around the cut-out.

Fit the fixing studs into the holes in the rear of the faceplate and tighten them with pliers. Slide them into position and check that the flap opens freely.

Fit the nuts and tighten them with your adjustable spanner. If the nuts are closed, shorten the bolts first with your hacksaw. If open, shorten afterwards.

Improving door security

Here are four simple and inexpensive DIY jobs you can do to make your front door more secure, especially if it has only a cylinder lock. Adding a five-lever mortise lock (*page 154*) will improve things even more.

you will need

→ Basic toolkit *plus*
→ 12 and 15mm (½ and ⅝in) diameter flat wood bits
→ 15 or 18mm (⅝ or ¾in) wood chisel
→ Extra bolts

Surface bolts

Fit surface-mounted bolts at the top and bottom of your front (and back) doors. If the screws supplied are less than 25mm (1in) long, substitute longer ones. You may have to chisel away a section of the door architrave in order to attach the keeper into which the bolt slides.

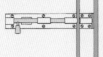

Door viewer

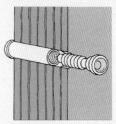

Fit a door viewer (also known as a fish-eye lens) to a solid front door so you can check the identity of callers before you open the door.

❶ Drill a hole – usually 12mm (½in) diameter – through the door at eye level. Take care not to splinter the wood as the drill breaks through the door.

❷ Push the barrel in from outside the door, then screw in the eyepiece from the inside. Use a slim coin to tighten it.

Door chain

This two-part device allows you to open the door a short way to check a caller's identity, but prevents an intruder from forcing the door open.

First fit the keeper to the door. Make pilot holes for the screws with a bradawl, then drive in the screws.

Mark where the chain part will fit on the door frame and screw it on. Chisel away the moulding if necessary so it fits flat.

Connect the chain to the keeper. Some types hook over it; others have a peg that fits in a slot.

Hinge bolts

These fixed bolts prevent the hinged edge of the door from being kicked in or forced open with a crowbar. Fit two, close to the top and bottom hinges.

1 Drill holes in the centre of the door edge to a depth of about 40mm (1⅝in). Tape around the drill bit indicates the hole depth.

2 Drive the ribbed end of each bolt into its hole. Close the door so each bolt marks the door frame.

3 Drill a 15mm (⅝in) hole 18mm (¾in) deep at each mark. Draw around the keeper, chisel out the recess and screw it on to the frame.

Fitting a mortise lock

If your door relies on just a cylinder rim lock for security, even if it is one that deadlocks and meets British Standard BS3621, you would be well advised to add a key-operated mortise lock lower down the door.

Choosing the lock

Make sure that the lock you choose is marked 'Made to British Standard BS3621' and carries the BS Kitemark. It should have five or, ideally, seven levers to make it almost impossible to pick.

1 Choose one with a recessed and reinforced metal keeper box.

2 Standard locks are 76mm (3in) deep, but you can buy shallower 64mm (2½in) ones for use in glazed doors with narrow sides (stiles).

3 Sashlocks combine a mortise lock and a latch, and are intended for use on side and back doors.

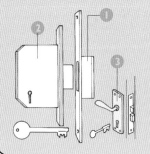

Forming the mortise

Mark the centre line of the door edge, then use the lock body to mark the top and bottom of the mortise – the slot that takes the lock.

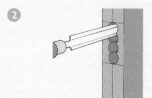

Use a flat wood bit a little wider than the lock body to drill overlapping holes along the centre line. Make them a little deeper than the lock depth. Then chisel out the waste to leave a rectangular slot.

Fitting the lock

   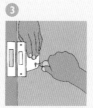 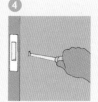

❶ Operate the lock so the bolt projects and push it into the slot. Use a knife to mark around the lock faceplate, then pull it out by gripping the bolt with pliers.

❷ Carefully chisel out the shallow recess in the door edge to accept the lock faceplate. Take care not to overshoot and damage the door.

❸ Hold the lock against the face of the door, lined up with its recess in the door edge, and mark the keyhole position with a bradawl. Drill a 10mm (⅜in) hole right through the door at this point.

❹ Then use a padsaw to make two parallel cuts down from the hole on each side of the door. Chop out the waste with a narrow chisel. Fit the lock and screw its faceplate to the door edge.

Fitting the keeper

  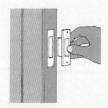

Fit escutcheons over the keyholes on both sides of the door. Then operate the lock and close the door so you can mark the position of the keeper on the frame.

Mark and chisel out the deep recess for the keeper box and the shallower one for its faceplate. Screw the keeper to the frame and test the operation of the lock.

Draughtproofing a front door

However well-fitting your front door, it will still admit draughts through the necessary clearance gaps between the door, the frame and the sill. Fitting draught excluders will solve the problem once and for all.

Choosing draught excluders

You need two different types of excluder to draughtproof a front door. The first stops gaps along the top and down the sides, while the second cuts draughts at sill level.

For the top and sides, self-adhesive foam strip excluders are the cheapest option. You simply stick them to the door frame. More expensive, but longer-lasting, are flexible-tube or brush excluders, which have a compressible seal held in a metal or plastic strip moulding. You pin or screw these to the frame so they press against the face of the door when it is closed. They are sold in kits of three lengths big enough to cope with all standard sized doors.

For the sill, the best excluders are sill-mounted, and press a flexible seal against the bottom edge of the door when it is closed. You generally need to shorten the door slightly. If this is beyond your DIY skills, fitting a screw-on brush or flexible-strip excluder to the base of the door on the inside will be better than nothing.

Sealing the top and sides

1

Stick foam strips to the stop beads on the lock edge and across the top. Stick the third strip so the hinged edge of the door compresses it as it closes.

2

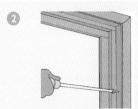

Screw flexible-tube and brush-type excluders to the door frame. Fit the top section first, then notch the top end of each side section to fit closely against the top section.

Sealing the sill

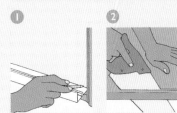
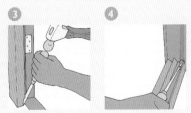

❶ Cut the excluder to length and hold it level with the sill so you can mark on the door face how much wood to remove from the bottom.

❷ Take the door off its hinges, lay it on your workbench and use a handsaw or power saw to remove the waste from the foot of the door. Paint or varnish the bare wood to stop damp penetrating.

❸ Offer up the excluder and mark where it meets the stop beads at each side. Chop away the wood and test the fit of the excluder, then rehang the door to check that it clears the excluder.

❹ Open the door and use mastic to bed excluder in place on the sill. Screw it down. Then add mastic to the two end blocks and screw these to the frame to make a watertight seal.

Screw-on door strip

As an alternative to a threshold seal, cut a brush or flexible strip excluder to length and screw it to the base of the door so the seal is against the sill.

Letter-box excluder

Complete the job of draughtproofing your door by screwing a bristle-type letter-box excluder to the inner face of the door. Some types have a neat flap to cover the bristles.

Windows: basic repairs

Most homes have wooden windows and, if looked after, they generally give a long and trouble-free life. The few everyday niggles that they can develop are all quick and easy to fix.

Casement windows

A casement window consists of an outer frame fixed to the masonry, with an assortment of fixed and hinged panes attached to it.

❶ The side-hung opening panes are called casements.

❷ Smaller top-hung panes are known as top vents.

❸ Stays and pins hold windows open for controlled ventilation.

Sash windows

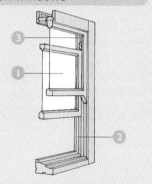

❶ A sash window consists of an outer frame containing two panes called sashes that slide up and down between guide beads fixed to the frame sides.

❷ Within the sides of the frame are two compartments containing the weights that counter-balance the sashes.

❸ The ropes that connect the two run over small pulleys at the top of each side of the frame.

Easing binding windows

①

Strip off the paint using a hot-air gun, then prime and repaint the bare wood. Take care not to strip adjacent surfaces.

②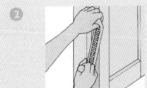

An alternative is to shave off the paint using a Surform planer file. Then sand the surface smooth ready for repainting.

③

Help sash windows to slide smoothly in their tracks by rubbing a candle on the sides of the frame and the inner surfaces of the guide beads.

Fixing a sagging casement

①

Cramp the sagging casement to the workbench and mark an L-shaped metal repair bracket at each frame corner.

②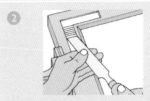

Chisel out a shallow recess for each bracket, taking care not to overshoot the recess and damage the casement.

③

Make pilot holes for the screws and fix the brackets in place. Apply filler over them, then rehang the casement.

Windows: more easy jobs

There are a couple of very simple jobs you can do to make your windows look better and work more efficiently. The first is to fit some new window furniture – catches and stays – and the second is to draughtproof them.

Fitting new furniture

   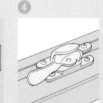

❶ On a casement window, remove the old stay and attach the new one. Place the locking pegs on the frame and fit the stay over them. Mark their positions, lift the stay aside and screw on the pegs.

❷ Screw the catch to the inner face of the opening casement. Close it and mark on the frame where the keeper will be positioned.

❸ Hold the keeper against its mark, make pilot holes for the screws and fix it to the frame. Test that it holds the window securely closed.

❹ On a sash window, replace the old catch with a fitch catch, which pulls the sashes together when operated and helps prevent rattles in windy weather.

Draughtproofing windows

Use self-adhesive rubber or foam excluder on casement windows. Stick a vertical strip to the inner face of the rebate into which the casement closes.

Stick two more strips in place at the top and bottom of the rebate. Cut each to size with scissors and form neat butt joints in the corners.

Complete the job by sticking the final strip to the side of the frame against which the hinged edge of the casement closes, not on the rebate like the others.

On sash windows, start by sticking a strip of self-adhesive rubber or foam excluder to the top and bottom of the frame against which the sashes close.

 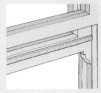

Stick a strip of self-adhesive brush excluder to the inner face of the meeting rail on the outer sash.

Pin lengths of rigid excluder with a bristle seal down each side of the sashes – on the inside of the inner sash as shown, and on the outside of the outer sash – so each can slide freely.

Mending a broken window

Windows get broken through all sorts of accident, from flying footballs to careless window cleaning. The first thing to do is to clear up the mess and make a temporary repair. Don't forget to wear thick gloves to prevent cuts from broken glass.

you will need

→ basic toolkit
→ thick gloves
→ glass repair tape
→ heavy-duty polythene
→ slim wood battens
→ old wood chisel *or* glazier's hacking knife
→ new glass
→ putty knife
→ putty
→ glazing sprigs

Temporary repairs

❶ If the glass is cracked, but not broken, make a temporary repair by sticking any sort of strong adhesive tape over the inside of the cracks to stop pieces falling out. Keep the window closed.

❷ If a small pane is broken, lift out loose pieces of glass and dispose of them in a cardboard box. Cut a piece of hardboard, thin plywood or MDF to fit the opening and fix it with panel pins.

❸ Make large panes weatherproof using heavy-duty polythene. Stick it to the frame with adhesive tape, then pin battens over the edges of the sheet to prevent it from tearing in the wind.

Measuring up

A pane of glass must not be a tight fit in its rebate, or movement in the frame could crack it. Measure the height and width of the rebate when you have removed all the old putty, and subtract 3mm (⅛in) from each measurement.

Ask your local glass merchant to cut the new pane to size for you. He will also supply putty and glazing sprigs, the small headless tacks that secure the pane in place. Allow about 125g (4oz) of putty per metre (yard) of rebate.

Fitting a new pane of glass

Lift out the broken glass. Then use a hammer and chisel or hacking knife to chip out all the old hard putty. Pull out any glazing sprigs with pliers.

 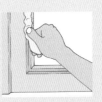

Take a lump of putty in your hand and begin to knead it to soften it. Then press a bed of putty all around the rebate with your thumb.

Offer up the new pane and press it into the bedding putty. Press along the edges, not in the centre of the pane. Aim to compress the putty to about 3mm (⅛in) thick.

 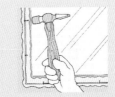

Secure the pane by tapping new glazing sprigs in at about 200mm (8in) intervals all around the rebate using a pin hammer.

Press more putty into the rebate to cover the edges of the glass and the sprigs. Form a neat 45° angle on the surface of this facing putty by drawing your putty knife over it.

Use an old paint brush to smooth the putty surface and bond it to the glass. Then go indoors and trim off the excess bedding putty flush with the frame.

Replacing sash cords

The biggest disaster that can happen to a sash window is one of the cords breaking. This will prevent the affected sash from staying open unless you jam it in place, and the only solution is to dismantle the window and replace the cord.

Removing the sashes

Even if only one sash cord has broken, it pays to replace them all while you have the window dismantled. Start by prising off the two mouldings (staff beads) that guide the inner sash.

 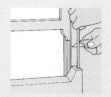

Cut through the unbroken cord just above the sash. Tie a knot in the cut end and let the weight down in its compartment until the knot jams in the pulley at the top of the frame.

Lift out the lower sash and remove the remains of the old cords from the grooves in the sides of the sash.

Prise the mouldings that separate the sashes (parting beads) from their grooves in the sides of the frame. If they have been painted over, free them at each side with a knife first. Then cut the cords and lift out the upper sash.

Replacing the cords

To get at the sash weights, locate and lever out the wooden covers (called pockets) at each side of the frame.

Lift out each weight in turn and label it (front left, etc). Then cut the knot off to release the weight and tie some string to the end of the old cord.

Pull the old cord out, tie new cord to the emerging string. Pull the new cord over the pulley and down the compartment. Tie one end to the weight and replace in its compartment. Repeat for other cords.

Rest the upper sash on the inside window ledge. Pull up each weight to the top of its compartment and wedge the cord in the pulley with a screwdriver. Nail the cords to the sides of the sash.

Remove the pulley wedges and push the sash up to check its action. Then tap the two parting beads back into their grooves at each side.

Repeat step 4 to attach the cords to the lower sash. Then replace the two staff beads and pin them to the frame. Fill any gaps and repaint the frame.

Fitting window locks 1

Good security is of major importance to householders everywhere, and fitting window locks is an easy way of making your home more burglar-proof. Most locks for casement windows can be fitted in minutes using just a few simple tools.

Locking catches

One of the simplest window locks you can fit is a locking catch that replaces the existing catch and keeper. Unscrew these, fit the new catch and keeper and lock it with the key supplied.

You can secure the catch on a metal window by screwing a lockable sliding bolt to the frame. Drill holes in the frame and attach the bolt with self-tapping screws. Push the case of the bolt up and lock it to secure the catch.

Stay locks

You can lock the casement stay in the closed or open position by replacing the standard stay pegs with special locking ones.

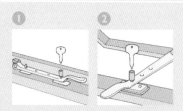

❶ Remove the existing stay pegs and screw on the locking peg so its pin fits through a hole in the stay. Screw the locknut on to the peg with the key.

❷ You can use this lock to secure the casement (or a top vent) in the open position for ventilation. Remove the locknut with the key, open the window and replace the locknut.

Push-button locks

Hold the assembled lock against the casement and frame, and mark its position on both surfaces.

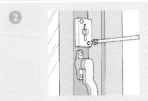

Separate the two parts of the lock, and screw the lock plate to the casement.

Screw the lock body to the frame. Fit the wedge supplied between it and the frame if the latter slopes. Close the window and push in the button to set the lock. Use the key to open it.

Swing-bar locks

❶ Screw the locking plate to the window frame. Close the window and hold the lock against the casement with the swing-bar over the locking plate. Mark its position, swing the bar aside and screw the lock to the casement.

❷ To operate the lock, move the swing-bar over the tongue on the locking plate and use the key to screw down the bar.

Mortise rack bolts

The mortise rack bolt fits in a hole drilled in the corner of the opening casement, and a special key is used to drive the bolt into a hole in the frame to lock the casement securely closed. It is best to fit one of these bolts at each corner of the casement.

Fitting window locks 2

If you have sliding sash windows, there are several types of lock you can use to make them more secure. Whichever you choose, it is best to fit two locks to each window – one at or near each side of the frame.

Dual screws

The dual screw is a threaded bolt that passes through the top rail of the lower sash and into the bottom rail of the upper one, locking them together when the sashes are closed.

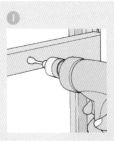  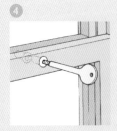

❶ Drill a 10mm (⅜in) diameter hole through the inner meeting rail, and on into the outer one to a depth of about 20mm (¾in). Wrap tape around the drill bit to show the total depth to drill.

❷ Tap the longer barrel into the hole in the lower sash, using a piece of scrap wood to protect the soft metal.

❸ Reverse the sash positions and tap the shorter barrel into the hole in the upper sash. Repeat steps 1 to 3 to fit a second pair of barrels at the other side of the sashes.

❹ Close the sashes, insert the bolts plain end first and use the key to screw the bolt in until its square head is flush with the sleeve in the lower sash.

Sash window stops

These devices prevent the sashes from passing each other, and a second pair can be positioned higher up to allow the window to be left slightly open for ventilation.

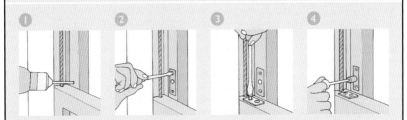

1 Drill a hole in the side of the upper sash, about 10mm (⅜in) above the top of the sash rail.

2 Hold the metal keeper over the hole and screw it into place. Repeat steps 1 and 2 at the other side of the window.

3 Screw a small protective metal plate to the top of the inner meeting rail at each side of the window.

4 Use the key supplied to screw the sash stop into the keeper. Repeat at the other side of the window.

Surface locks

These are a quick-fit alternative to dual screws or sash stops. Screw one part of the lock to each meeting rail and use the key supplied to turn the locking bolt until it engages in the outer block.

Emergency security

If you do not have any locks on your sash windows and you are going away on holiday with no time to fit them, screw the meeting rails together. Drill a clearance hole in the inner rail and drive a No 12 screw through into the outer rail.

Cleaning and patching carpets

Carpets are still the most popular floorcovering for most rooms in the house. Things get spilt on them or trodden into them. And sometimes they actually become torn or frayed through excess wear.

Dealing with stains

When something gets dropped on a carpet, deal with it very quickly.

• Scrape up solids and thick liquids with a spoon or a knife.

• Blot up liquids with wads of tissue or kitchen roll. Lay a pad over the stain and tread on it to get maximum pressure and extract as much liquid as possible.

• Remove what remains of the stain using the correct cleaning agent. Use carpet shampoo on water-based stains such as soft drinks, alcohol, jam, ketchup, blood and urine. Use dry-cleaning solvent for grease-based stains such as cooking oil, gravy, milk and ice cream.

• Apply shampoo or solvent sparingly, using just enough on a cloth to treat the affected area. Turn the cloth frequently so you absorb more of the stain each time. Work from the outside of the stained area towards the centre to avoid spreading it further.

Specific stain treatments

• **Ball-point pen.** Dab with methylated spirits on a cotton wool bud.

• **Candlewax.** Scrape off as much as possible. Cover remains with a pad of kitchen roll and iron over it so the wax is absorbed by the paper. Remove final traces with dry-cleaning solvent.

• **Chewing gum.** Freeze gum with proprietary aerosol spray and scrape off solidified remains.

• **Curry.** Mop up as much as possible, then clean area with borax solution (15ml borax per 500ml of water). Sponge with warm water and blot dry.

• **Felt-tip pen.** Use methylated spirit on a cotton bud on spirit-based inks, and carpet shampoo for water-based ones.

• **Paint.** Scrape off as much as possible. Mop up emulsion paint stains with wet cloths. Use white spirit to dilute solvent-based paint stains and blot off with pads of tissue. Seek professional help for dealing with large spillages, or claim replacement on your insurance.

Patching damaged carpet

If an area of carpet has become badly worn, frayed or otherwise damaged – by a cigarette burn, for example – the best solution is to patch it. Use an offcut if you were practical enough to save any when the carpet was originally laid. Otherwise cut a patch from underneath a piece of fitted or seldom-moved furniture and use that for the repair.

1 Hold the patch over the damaged area with the pile running in the same direction. Cut through patch and carpet along all four sides with your knife.

2 Brush latex carpet adhesive round the edges of the hole in the carpet and on the edges of the patch, to about half-way up the pile. This will stop the cut edges from fraying.

3 Cut four strips of carpet tape, and stick them to the underside of the carpet beneath each edge of the hole. Peel off the release tape and press each edge of the hole down firmly on to the tape.

4 Insert the patch with the pile facing the same way as the carpet and press it down firmly. Then hammer the carpet down along all the joins. Finally fluff up the pile to conceal them.

5 On foam-backed carpet, roll back the carpet, lay the patch in place and stick it to the foam with lengths of carpet tape. Replace the carpet and hammer the edges of the patch as in step 4.

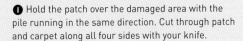

Removing old floorcoverings

There comes a time when every floorcovering reaches the end of its useful life... or you may simply be fed up with the look of it. Either way, it needs replacing and that means you have to get it off the floor.

Fitted carpet

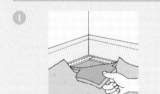

Cut the old carpet near room corners so you can lift flaps and get a good grip. Pull the carpet away from the gripper strips all around.

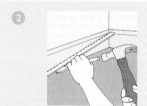

Always discard old underlay if you are putting down a new carpet. If you are laying another floorcovering, prise up all the gripper strips with a bolster and hammer and remove fixing nails.

Wood floors

❶ Prise up woodblock panel floors, section by section, using an old, wide chisel and a hammer or mallet. Leave traditional parquet floors in place; they were laid on bitumen adhesive and are extremely difficult to remove.

❷ Lift loose-laid interlocking laminate floors by starting at the edge with the last cut-down strip. Drive screws into the strip at intervals and use pliers to grip them and lift it out. Then work back across the floor, prising strips apart and lifting them.

❸ Glued laminate flooring is impossible to lift without damaging the planks. Use a circular saw to cut across and along the planks so you can prise up sections of the flooring.

Sheet vinyl

Prise up the sheet at a seam or in a room corner. With luck, only the seams and edges will have been stuck down.

Peel back the vinyl, using a scraper to free it from the adhesive. Cut it into strips, roll them up and carry them out.

If the vinyl has been stuck down all over, lift and tear back a corner or seam. Push a garden spade underneath the vinyl and lift it section by section.

Vinyl and cork tiles

Investigate how the tiles have been stuck down. If they are stuck to a solid concrete floor, lifting them will be extremely difficult. If they are well stuck down, it is better to leave them and lay your new floorcovering over the top.

If the tiles were laid on a wooden floor with a hardboard underlay, you should be able to prise the entire sandwich up. Start work in a room corner, breaking up the tiles and the hardboard. Then pull up the hardboard sheets with the tiles still stuck to them. You can use a garden spade to lift them, as described for sheet vinyl.

Ceramic and quarry tiles

There is no quick way of lifting these. Remove the door threshold strip to create a starting point, then break out the tiles one by one using a brick bolster and club hammer. You will probably have to level the floor surface afterwards (see pages 184–185).

Fixing floor faults

When you have lifted your old floorcovering, give the floor surface underneath a quick once-over. This is the perfect opportunity to deal with cracked and dusty concrete, and warped or squeaking floorboards.

Timber floors

Check the floor surface for raised nail heads, which indicate that boards are loose. Punch in to a depth of about 3mm (⅛in) with a nail punch and hammer.

If the nails will not hold the boards down, screw them firmly. Drill a clearance hole close to each failed nail and countersink it.

Drive the screws in until their heads sit deep in their countersinks and pull the boards tightly against the joists below. Use cross-head screws and drive them with a power screwdriver.

 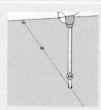

On chipboard floors, drive in extra screws to stop the boards from creaking. Locate every joist the board crosses by test drilling, then drive in screws at 150mm (6in) intervals.

Concrete floors

 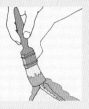

Brush dust and debris out of any cracks. Then wet the crack with water to stop the filler from drying too quickly.

Fill the cracks with a sand/cement mortar mix or masonry filler. Press into the cracks and trowel it smooth.

Chop out loose concrete from larger areas of damage, using a brick bolster and club hammer. Brush and vacuum-clean the area to remove dust.

To ensure that damp cannot rise at the damaged area, treat the inside of the hole with two coats of bituminous damp-proofing solution.

When the damp-proofer has dried, fill the hole with sand/cement mortar, packing it down well and levelling it with a trowel or plasterer's float.

Seal dusty concrete floors with a coat of diluted PVA building adhesive. Put it on with a paint roller. Use an extension pole so you can do the job standing up.

Replacing a floorboard

Plumbers and electricians are floorboards' biggest enemies. Whenever they have to lift a board to gain access to pipes or cables in the floor void, they often split it and usually fail to fix it back down properly. Replacement is the only option.

Lifting a square-edged board

1 If the damaged board is loose, simply lift it out. Otherwise lever up one end of the board with the aid of a bolster chisel.

2 Wedge the bolster under the end of the board to keep it raised. Use a claw hammer under the board edges to lever up the rest of the board.

Lifting a tongued-and-grooved board

Check if you have tongued-and-grooved boards by inserting a knife blade between the planks. If you have, use a floorboard saw (1) to cut through the tongues at each side of the board.

If you have a circular saw, you can use this instead to sever the tongues (2). Set the cutting depth to 15mm (⅝in) so you do not damage cables or pipes below.

Cutting out a section

If you cannot lift a whole board, you will have to cut across it. Locate the nearest joist by looking for the fixing nails in the board, and drill a 10mm (⅜in) diameter hole in the board about 25mm (1in) away from the nail heads so it just clears the joist. Then insert the blade of your jigsaw in the hole and cut across the board. Lift the board by inserting a bolster chisel in the cut and prising it up.

Fitting the new board

If you are replacing a whole board, cut it to length and plane off its tongue so you can lay it in place on its joists. Nail it down to each joist it crosses.

If you are replacing just a short section, you must provide some support for the end next to the joist. Screw an offcut of wood to its side.

Cut the new board to length and plane off its tongue. Hammer it into place against its neighbour using a wood offcut to protect its edge. Then tap it down flat and nail it into place.

If you do not have a plane to remove the board tongue, clamp the board in your workbench and use a chisel to shave it off.

Replacing skirting boards

If you are giving a room a complete makeover, and your existing skirting boards are dated, scuffed and clogged with years of old paint, replacing them with new mouldings will greatly enhance the room's appearance.

you will need

→ basic toolkit
→ crowbar
→ coping saw
→ mitre saw jig

Choosing skirting boards

There is a wide range of skirting board styles available, from plain splayed-and-rounded types to more ornate period profiles. Most skirting boards are softwood, and you will find the biggest choice at your local timber merchant.

Many DIY superstores also stock MDF mouldings. These have two big advantages over softwood types. They are already primed, ready for painting, and they are free from the usual blemishes that affect softwood boards, such as warps and knots.

Removing the old boards

On masonry walls, the boards will have been fixed with big cut nails. Lever them off with a crowbar. Place some scrap wood between the tool and the wall.

On timber-framed walls, the boards will be pinned on. Insert a wide chisel behind each section and prise it off.

Fitting the new boards

If possible, cut a piece long enough to reach the next corner. Use masonry nails on solid walls, wire on timber-framed ones.

Scribe the board profile on to the end of the next length so it will fit neatly around the board on the first wall.

Use a coping saw to cut along the marked line, rotating the blade as necessary to follow any curves. Offer up the board and nail it into place.

Cut mitres for external corners – at chimney breasts, for example. Use a jigsaw with the baseplate set at 45°, or use a mitre saw jig (see page 17).

Glue external mitres to stop the joint from opening up, and drive panel pins into the joint from opposite sides.

On timber-framed walls where the plasterboard presents a flat, true surface, you can stick skirting boards on with quick-grip adhesive.

Sanding a floor

If you have planked floors that are in good condition, sanding and sealing them is an economical and attractive alternative to putting down a new floorcovering. You can hire the sanders and buy the abrasives from your local plant hire shop.

you will need

→ floor sander (hired)
→ abrasive sheets
→ edge sander (hired)
→ abrasive discs
→ finishing sander

Preparing the floor

A floor sander will strip off old paint, stain or varnish from the floorboards with ease. What will wreck the expensive abrasive sheets are any projecting nail heads. Therefore, it is essential to go over the entire floor surface and punch in all the floorboard nails to a depth of about 3mm (⅛in).

If screws have been used to secure any boards, drive them in so their heads are below the board surface and fill the recesses with matching wood stopper.

Fitting the abrasives

The floor sander uses abrasive sheets, fitted to its rotating drum and secured by a screw-down gripper bar. Loosen this and tuck both ends of a coarse sheet under it. Check that the sheet is taut, then tighten the gripper bar screws.

The edge sander uses abrasive discs, secured by a centre nut and washer. Use the key supplied with the tool to tighten the nut fully.

Sanding the floor

Raise the drum, start the motor, then lower it to the floor and let the machine move forward. Work diagonally.

Switch to a medium abrasive sheet and sand the floor along the direction of the boards. Then use a fine abrasive sheet.

At each end of the room, run the sander across the line of the boards as close to the skirting board as you can.

Fit a coarse disc to the edging sander and guide it along the skirting boards to sand the perimeter of the floor. Repeat with medium and then fine abrasive.

Use a finishing sander or a hand sanding block to sand corners and areas such as around radiator pipes where the big sanders cannot reach.

Safety first

The wood dust created by the sander is very hot, and can ignite spontaneously if it is also impregnated with old stain, varnish or paint. To prevent this, empty the machine's dust bag into an open container, and allow the dust to cool before bagging it up.

Decorative floor finishes

Once you have sanded your floorboards, you can apply any one of several decorative finishes – varnish, wood stain or paint. Varnish and wood stain will enhance the colour and grain of the wood, while paint makes for some interesting colour effects.

Using varnish

Always thin the first coat of varnish to help it to penetrate the wood. Thin polyurethane varnish with white spirit and acrylic varnish with water.

Use a knife to lift out any loose debris from between the floorboards that could spoil the finish. Then vacuum the floor to remove dust.

Apply the first thinned coat of varnish with a brush, working along the direction of the wood grain, finishing one plank before moving to the next.

Once the first coat has dried hard, key the surface and remove any specks of dust by rubbing it with a pad of fine wire wool moistened with white spirit. Then apply a second full-strength coat.

Using wood stain

Test the effect of the stain on an offcut of wood before you apply it.

Apply the stain with a pad of lint-free cloth, wiping the stain along the direction of the wood grain. Try not to create overlaps, which will show as a patch of a deeper colour. If you want to stain adjoining boards a different colour, hold a piece of card between the two boards to prevent the colour from spreading.

TIP

Control the depth of colour of wood stain more effectively by applying two or three thin coats rather than one thick coat.

Using paint

Stick masking tape to the skirting boards all around the room. Then apply a generous coat of wood primer.

When the primer is dry, use a brush to apply a neat band of floor paint around the perimeter of the room.

Switch to a roller with an extension pole to paint the main body of the floor. Roll with the grain to begin with, then across it to fill the joints.

Levelling a floor

Old concrete floors are often quite uneven, while old floorboards often have raised edges and gaps between the boards, which will show through soft floorcoverings such as sheet vinyl and flexible tiles. They need levelling.

Levelling a concrete floor

Self-smoothing compound is a powder sold in bags that you mix with water. Some come with liquid latex or acrylic additives that help prevent cracking. A 25kg (55lb) bag will make enough compound to cover about 7sq m (8sq yd).

To contain the runny compound, pin timber battens across door openings. Vacuum the floor to lift dust.

Mix the compound by adding powder to water in a bucket. Take care to break up any lumps, then mix in any additives.

Pour out the mixed compound in the corner farthest from the door, covering about 1sq m (1sq yd) at a time.

Use a wooden float or a metal trowel to spread the compound to a thickness of about 5mm (¼in).

Levelling a timber floor

Use 1200 x 610mm (4 x 2ft) sheets of 3mm (⅛in) hardboard to cover the boards – they are easier to handle than full-sized sheets. Fix the sheets with 19mm (¾in) long annular (ring-shank) nails.

Start work in a corner, butting the first sheet against the skirting. Nail it at 150mm (6in) intervals along the edges and across the centre.

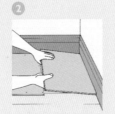

Lay further sheets in the same way. At the end of the row, cut the last one down in size to fit the gap.

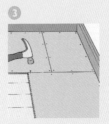

Use the offcut from the first row to start the second row, so that the joints between sheets will be staggered.

Lay a sheet over the last one laid and butt another on top against the skirting board. Mark a line on the middle sheet, cut along it and fit the offcut in the gap.

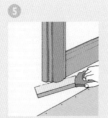

At door openings, use a tenon saw to trim the foot of the architrave and slip the edge of the sheet underneath it.

Mark radiator pipe positions and drill a 16mm (⅝in) diameter hole at each mark. Then saw in from the edge to form a notch that will fit around the pipe.

Laying woodstrip flooring

Woodstrip (laminate) flooring is one of the most popular floor finishes. It can be laid quickly over existing timber or concrete floors, and the latest lock-together types need no adhesive.

Preparation

On timber floors, punch down protruding nails and fix loose boards securely. On solid floors, fill obvious depressions with mortar and allow to dry hard. See page 175 for techniques of repairing concrete floors and page 184 for how to level a solid floor.

Unroll the foam underlay; staple it to timber floors, tape it to solid ones. On uneven floors, use thicker felt underlay boards.

Laying the first row

❶ Start laying planks against the longest wall in the room, with the short-tongue edge facing in. Fit spacers as shown.

❷ Locate the short tongue of the second plank into the long tongue of the first, and lower it to lock it into place.

❸ Finish the row with a cut-to-length plank. Reverse a whole plank, add a spacer and mark the length as shown.

Completing the floor

Start the next row with the offcut. Lock the long edges of the planks first, then use a tamping block to close the joints.

Continue laying planks row by row. Use a pulling bar and hammer as shown to close the final joint in each row.

Use two whole planks positioned as shown to mark the width of the edge strip on the lower plank. Cut and fit it.

Fitting and finishing

At radiator pipes, offer up and mark the board. Draw the slot, drill a 16mm (⅝in) hole at the end and saw out.

At doorways, lay a plank by the frame, rest a saw on it and cut through the architrave. Fit the plank under it.

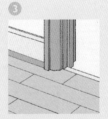

Finish the floor by gluing quadrant trim to the skirting boards. Add a threshold bar to finish the doorway.

Laying ceramic and quarry tiles

Ceramic and quarry tiles are a popular choice of floorcovering for rooms such as kitchens, hallways and conservatories. They are cold underfoot unless you have under-floor heating, but they provide an extremely hard-wearing surface.

Setting out the floor

Find the centres of two facing walls and draw a chalk line across the floor between them. Dry-lay tiles at right angles to this line, with spacers between them, up to one wall. If you are left with a gap of less then half a tile's width, move the line to one side by half a tile's width. Repeat for the other direction. Mark the positions of the last whole tiles in each row as a guide for placing the edge battens.

On timber floors, give the tiles a solid base by screwing down sheets of 9mm (⅜in) exterior-grade plywood. Fit them as described on page 185 (Levelling a timber floor). If you do not do this, movement in the floorboards will soon crack the tiles.

Fixing the guide battens

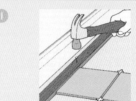

When you have set out the tile rows to your satisfaction, nail a timber guide batten by the wall furthest from the door. Use masonry nails on a solid floor, wire nails on a plywood overlay.

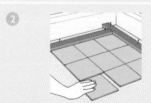

Fix a second batten at right angles to the first one, and check the angle by dry-laying nine tiles in the corner.

Laying the tiles

Spread enough adhesive to lay about 1sq m (1sq yd). The ridges in the adhesive help bed each tile to the same level.

 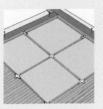

Then place tiles one by one, and fit spacers at all the intersections. Bed them well into the adhesive.

Check that the tiles are level with their neighbours by placing a long spirit level across them. Continue laying whole tiles until you reach the room door.

Allow the adhesive to set for 24 hours. Then prise up the battens and fit the edge tiles. Use a cutting jig for ceramic tiles, a power tile saw for quarry tiles.

Spread adhesive on the back of each cut piece and bed it in place. Cut and fit all the edge tiles in the same way, finishing off with a piece in the corner.

Fill the joints with waterproof grout. Force it in and scrape off excess as you work. When it has set, polish off smears with a coarse dry cloth.

Laying sheet vinyl

Sheet vinyl is an ideal floorcovering for kitchens and bathrooms, where you want a seamless, water-resistant surface. It is available in a huge range of designs and colourways, and is simply stuck down at the edges with double-sided tape.

Laying vinyl in large rooms

Unroll the vinyl and crease it into the corners. Trim off all but about 50mm (2in) from each edge. Make a triangular cut across each corner so the sheet lies flat.

Crease the vinyl along one wall into the angle. Press it down with a steel straight-edge and cut it with a sharp knife. Repeat for the other three walls.

If the room has an alcove, start a cut at 45° to the external corner, then cut straight and parallel with the side wall of the alcove. This creates a trim allowance along that wall.

Push the flap into the alcove, ready for trimming, and cut off the excess vinyl along the wall next to the external corner. Then cut and trim it as in step 2.

Laying vinyl in bathrooms

It is much harder to lay sheet vinyl in a bathroom because of the various obstacles in the way – basin pedestals and WCs in particular. The solution is to make a paper template of the floor plan and to use that to cut the sheet exactly to fit.

Lay paper on the floor, taping sheets together and cutting them to fit roughly around the various obstacles. Tape the template to the wall.

Tape a felt-tip pen to a small block of wood. Press the block against each obstacle. Move it along marking the outline on the template.

Tape the template to the vinyl. Move the block along the inside of the lines around the obstacles to scribe their actual size on to the vinyl.

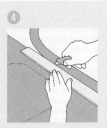

Move the block along the outside of the room outline on the template to scribe the actual room size on to the vinyl. Cut along the lines with a sharp knife.

Cut the vinyl around each obstacle. Then make a slit between each cut-out and the edge of the sheet so you can fit it around the obstacle.

With all the cuts complete, stick double-sided tape to the floor all round the room and around each obstacle. Lay the sheet in place and press it down.

Laying carpet: the basics

Laying carpet is not difficult, especially if you plan to put down foam-backed carpet that needs no underlay and can be stuck down at the edges. Hessian-backed carpet has to be stretched once laid, and is hooked on to toothed gripper strips at the edges.

you will need

→ carpet
→ gripper strips *or*
→ double-sided
   adhesive tape
→ door threshold
   strips
→ clean bolster
   chisel
→ basic toolkit

Preparing the floor

If you are laying foam-backed carpet, stick double-sided tape all around the perimeter of the room. Leave the release paper on for now.

For hessian-backed carpet, nail gripper strips around the room. Set them in by 10mm (⅜in) so the edges of the carpet can be tucked into the gaps.

Cut lengths of underlay to fit between the gripper strips and staple them to the floorboards. Tape the seams and edges instead on solid floors.

Laying hessian-backed carpet

1 Cut the carpet about 100mm (4in) bigger than the size of the room. Align one edge with the longest wall and let it lap up the skirting boards at each end. Press the long edge on to the grippers.

2 Trim one end of the carpet to size. Push the knife blade in at a 45° angle to the skirting board and cut between it and the gripper strip. Press the cut edge down on to the grippers. Stretch the carpet across the room. Shuffle your feet across the room in both directions, and press the untrimmed edges on to the grippers.

3 Cut off the corner of the carpet at the untrimmed corner so it will lie flat. Then trim the other two walls as in step 2. Tuck the cut edges into the gap between the skirting board and the gripper strip with a bolster chisel.

4 At a chimney breast, unroll the carpet to meet it and make cuts from the back in line with the sides of the alcoves. Let the tongues fall into the alcoves and trim the excess carpet across the front.

Laying foam-backed carpet

Follow the same basic technique for laying foam-backed carpet, cutting off corners to let the carpet lie flat and then trimming it to size. Make sure the knife is pressed hard into the angle between floor and skirting board, to ensure that the carpet is a good fit. With all the trimming complete, lift the edges and peel the release paper from the tape. Bed the carpet on to the tape with foot pressure for a good bond.

Laying stair carpet: the basics

This sounds like a difficult job, but on a straight flight it is actually easier than carpeting a room. The secret is to use gripper strips in the angles between the treads and risers, and at the sides of the treads, to hold the carpet securely in place.

Preparing the stairs

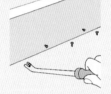

Remove the old stair carpet and underlay pads, and prise out any old tacks with a tack lifter. While the stairs are bare, do any necessary repairs.

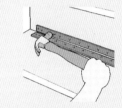

Cut pieces of gripper strip to the width of the treads less about 40mm (1⅝in). Nail them to the treads first. Then nail strips to the risers, with teeth pointing down.

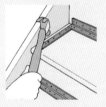

Cut short pieces of gripper strip and nail these to the sides of the treads. Leave a 12mm (½in) gap at the sides and a 25mm (1in) gap at the front.

Cut pieces of underlay long enough to cover each tread and the riser below it, and wide enough to fit between the side gripper strips. Staple them on.

Laying the carpet

With broadloom carpet, cut strips to match the width of the flight. Tack the top of the strip to the face of the top riser.

Unroll the strip down the flight, fitting it between the sides and tucking it roughly into the shapes of the treads and risers.

Use a clean bolster chisel and a hammer to force the carpet into the angle between the two gripper strips at the back of each tread.

If you need more than one strip of carpet, trim the lower end of the first strip at the bottom of a riser and press it against its gripper strip.

Start the next strip by pressing it on to the gripper strip at the back of the next tread. Then trim it to finish at the bottom of the last riser.

Use your brick bolster to tuck the edges of the carpet into the gaps between the side gripper strips and the staircase sides to finish the job.

Fixing creaky stairs

The staircase is one of the most complex pieces of joinery in the house, and it can develop a few creaks and groans as it gets older. Because its structure is usually hidden, carrying out any necessary repairs requires a few clever tricks.

Working from above

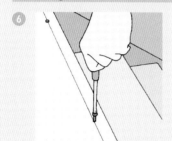

you will need

→ woodworking adhesive
→ steel angle repair brackets
→ 38mm long screws
→ triangular blocks

1 If you cannot gain access to the underside of the staircase, you will have to remove the stair carpet. Then prise open any creaky joints with a chisel.

2 Run a bead of woodworking adhesive along the joint so it can trickle down into the gap and stick it closed. Keep off the stairs while it sets.

3 Reinforce creaky joints by screwing a pair of steel angle repair brackets into the tread-riser angle. They will be hidden when you replace the carpet.

4 If the front of a tread creaks, measure the overhang of its nosing and add 5mm (¼in) to this. Mark a pencil line across this tread at this distance from the edge of the nosing.

5 Drill and countersink three or four evenly spaced clearance holes in the tread along the pencil line.

6 Drive 38mm (1½in) long screws into each of the holes to lock the tread and riser together. Repeat for any other creaky treads.

Working from below

1

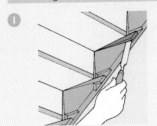

If you can gain access to the underside of the staircase – via an under-stairs cupboard, for example – check that the wedges holding the treads and risers to the staircase sides (the strings) are tight. If any are loose, prise them out.

2

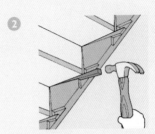

Apply some PVA woodworking adhesive to each loose wedge and hammer it back into place. The short vertical wedges go in first, and are held in place by the longer horizontal ones.

3

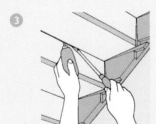

Prise open the joint between each creaky tread and its riser with a screwdriver, and squirt woodworking adhesive into the joint.

4

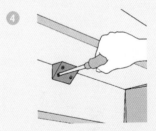

Glue and screw triangular blocks of wood into the tread-riser angle to provide extra reinforcement.

Repairing a damaged stair tread

The easiest way to damage a stair tread is to drop a piece of heavy furniture on it, especially on the nosing at the front of the tread. This may splinter a softwood tread and break away a chunk of an MDF one. Here's how to fix the problem.

Removing the damage

Roll back the stair carpet and remove the underlay. Use a hammer and chisel to chop away the damaged wood flush with the face of the riser below.

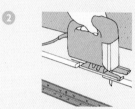

Hold your jigsaw with its blade flush with the face of the riser. Cut the tread for about 75mm (3in) beyond the damaged area in each direction.

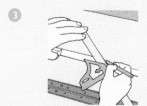

Mark cutting lines at 45° to the edge of the tread using a combination square so that the lines intersect with the saw cuts made in step 2.

Use the jigsaw again to make two angled cuts into the edge of the tread. Remove the waste wood.

Patching the nosing

Buy a length of tread nosing moulding from a timber merchant. If you cannot obtain this, you can use a softwood offcut instead and shape it later.

Use a Surform planer file to smooth any irregularities in the saw cut you made across the tread, so the rear face of the cut-out is flush with the riser.

Hold a length of the moulding beneath the cut-out in the tread and mark the positions of the mitre cuts on it. Cut the mitres on the moulding.

Drill and countersink holes through the moulding at 150mm (6in) intervals. Apply adhesive to its rear face and both ends.

Fit the moulding and align it with the top surface of the tread. Drive in the fixing screws and wipe away excess adhesive.

Replacing a tread

If the main part of the tread is split, you will have to fit a replacement tread. This involves cutting through the tongues between the tread and the risers above and below it, removing the wedges from below the staircase and hammering out the tread from above. Slide the replacement in from below and screw it to the two risers. Leave the job to a carpenter if you are unsure.

Repairing a balustrade

A staircase balustrade is a major safety feature, designed to stop anyone using the stairs from falling into the stairwell. If you trip on the stairs and fall against it, or move furniture carelessly, it is easy to damage individual balusters.

you will need

→ woodworking adhesive
→ strong adhesive tape
→ new baluster
→ 50mm (2in) nails
→ clamp
→ basic toolkit

Temporary repairs

If you crack or split a baluster, repair it temporarily by squeezing woodworking adhesive into the split and binding the baluster with strong adhesive tape.

Removing a baluster

❶ If the baluster is badly damaged, pull the two sections apart. Lever the top end away from the underside of the handrail, and the bottom end out of the top edge of the staircase side (string).

❷ If you cannot free the broken baluster in this way, hold it firmly and cut through it with a hand saw. Take care not to damage neighbouring balusters.

❸ The ends of the balusters are spaced by small pieces of wood called fillets. Use a chisel to prise out the fillet below the bottom of the old baluster and the other above the top.

Fitting the new baluster

Buy a matching baluster. Use one end of the old baluster to mark the first cutting angle on one end of the new baluster.

Measure the height of the baluster from a baluster next to the damaged one. Mark and cut the new piece to length.

Slot the top end of the baluster into the gap in the underside of the handrail and drive in a 50mm (2in) nail. Hold it with pliers and hammer on the jaws.

 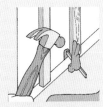

Clamp the base of the baluster against the fillet above it and nail it to the staircase side. Drive the nail at an angle so you can hammer and punch it home.

Replace the fillet between the base of the baluster and its neighbour. Do not glue it in; just pin it in place.

Replace the fillet between the top end of the baluster and its neighbour. Pin it to the underside of the handrail.

Replacing a balustrade

This used to be a job to leave to a skilled carpenter. However, you can now buy a kit of parts that makes the job of fitting a new balustrade to an existing staircase a relatively straightforward job.

you will need

→ newel posts

→ balusters

→ balustrade kit

→ woodworking adhesive

→ basic toolkit

TIP

If you are replacing the newel posts, fit them first, following the step-by-step instructions carefully. They must be secure, as they support the entire balustrade.

Choosing components

A staircase balustrade consists of three main components:

• newel posts fitted at each end and at changes of direction

• handrails linking each pair of newel posts

• balusters that fit between the handrail and the side of the staircase (or the landing floor).

Balustrade kits also include a base rail to fit on the staircase side, spacing fillets to fit between the balusters, and special brackets to connect the handrail to the new posts.

Replace the newel posts only if you want them to match the style of the new balustrade. Replacement newels are attached by drilling a large-diameter hole in the stub of the old post and gluing them into place.

Removing the old balustrade

1 Begin by sawing through each baluster in turn. Take care not to damage the newel posts at each end of the balustrade if you are keeping them.

2 Wrench the two halves of each baluster out – they are usually secured by one nail at each end. Prise out the old fillets (*page 200*) if this helps.

3 Remove the old handrail by undoing its fixing screws. If a bracket was used to attach it to the newel post, locate the screw heads in the underside of the rail and undo them to free it.

Fitting the new parts

Read the instructions supplied with the balustrade kit before you start work, and check that you have all the parts you need.

1 Prise off the existing base rail and replace it with the new one. Use the old rail as a template for cutting the new one to length and angling its ends.

2 Similarly, use the old handrail as a template for the new one. Get someone to support it while you fit it. Attach it with two 75mm (3in) screws or the special bracket if supplied.

3 Fit the first baluster at the top of the staircase, after pinning on fillets at top and bottom to space it away from the newel post. Nail it at top and bottom, then repeat for the other balusters.

Putting up a shelf

Everyone needs shelves, and putting them up is the second most popular DIY project after home decorating. It is a job that must be done well if the shelves are to stay put and not sag alarmingly as soon as they are on the wall.

Shelves and brackets

• If shelves are not to sag, three things are important – the shelf material, its thickness and the spacing of the brackets. The heavier the load, the thicker the shelf should be. Heavily-laden shelves may need more than two brackets, and may also need some extra reinforcement.

• Natural timber and plywood make the strongest shelves, while chipboard and MDF tend to sag under load. As a general guide, use shelves at least 18mm (¾in) thick for books and hi-fis.

• The simplest way of checking if a new shelf is strong enough is to rest it on two narrow supports and load it up with whatever you want it to carry. Place a straight-edge along the front of the shelf to see if it is sagging. If it is, move the support positions closer together, add an extra support or increase the shelf thickness.

• Glass shelves need brackets at 400mm (16in) intervals for 6mm (¼in) glass, and at 600mm (24in) for 9mm (¾in) heavy-duty shelving.

Fixing the brackets

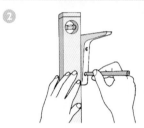

❶ When you have chosen your shelf and decided on the correct bracket spacing, use a spirit level and pencil to mark a light pencil line on the wall where the shelf is to go.

❷ Mark the bracket positions on the line. Then hold each bracket in place and mark the position of the top screw hole. Drill and plug this, and screw the bracket to the wall. Check that the bracket is vertical and mark the bottom fixing hole. Swing the bracket out of the way, drill and plug the hole, and fit the second screw.

Fixing the shelf

❷ Place the shelf on the brackets with an equal overhang at each end. Hold the shelf down and use a bradawl to mark through the holes for the fixing screws.

❸ Lift the shelf off and drill pilot holes at each mark. Replace the shelf and screw each bracket to it. Use short screws so they do not pierce the top of the shelf.

Expanding metal anchors see page 25.

❶ Screw the brackets to the wall with 50mm (2in) screws. On hollow walls, use expanding metal anchors.

Fitting a stack of shelves

For several shelves, one above the other, fix vertical battens to the wall first and screw the brackets to that – quicker than making a lot of individual wall fixings.

Place the battens side by side and mark the bracket positions on them. Drill and countersink the fixing holes, and screw the battens to the wall.

Make pilot holes for the bracket screws with a bradawl and screw the brackets to the battens. Rest each shelf on its brackets and mark the batten positions on it.

Make two saw cuts into the edge of the shelf at the marks. Then chop out the waste wood with a chisel. Replace the shelf and screw the brackets to it.

Putting shelves in an alcove

Alcoves are a natural place to put shelves, whether it is for display purposes or to house your library or your sound system. Their shape allows you to use the alcove walls to support the shelves.

Preparing the battens

Alcove shelving is supported by battens fixed to the side walls, level with each other. You can add a third batten on the back wall to give the shelf extra support if it will have to carry heavy loads, such as books. Use 38 x 19mm (1½ x ⅜in) battens, fixed to the walls with 50mm (2in) screws driven into wall plugs. Most alcoves have solid walls because they flank a chimney breast, but if you have a timber-framed wall next to the alcove, use expanding metal anchors (see page 25) to make the fixings.

you will need

→ basic toolkit
→ shelves
→ 38 x 19mm (1½ x ⅜in) battens
→ 50mm (2in) screws
→ wall plugs

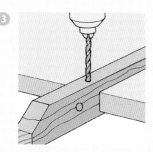

❶ Measure up for the battens. Cut one for the back wall 10mm (⅜in) less than the alcove width, and two for the sides 50mm (2in) shorter than the shelf width.

❷ Trim a triangle off the end of each batten using a mitre box. This helps conceal the ends of the battens when the shelf is in place.

❸ Drill and countersink two holes through each side batten and three through the back batten. If you plan to screw the battens to the shelf, drill two holes through the depth of the side battens, offset from the first holes.

Fitting the shelf

If you need a batten on the back wall, position it with a spirit level on top, and mark the positions of the screws. Drill and plug the holes, then attach the batten.

Hold each side batten level with the back one, and mark the fixing holes as before. Drill and plug the holes and fix the batten in place.

Check whether the alcove corners are square by holding a try square in each of them. If they are, measure the alcove width and cut the shelf to length.

Rest the shelf on the battens and secure it with screws driven up through the battens from below.

Coping with awkward alcoves

Sometimes alcoves are seriously out of square, and a shelf with square-cut ends will not fit. Use a sliding bevel to record the corner angle. Open its blade, hold the wooden part against the back wall and press the blade against the side wall.

Lock it in that position, place it on the shelf and mark the angle of the side wall on it. Cut this end of the shelf. Then measure the alcove width at front and back, transfer these measurements to the shelf and cut the other end to fit.

Putting up track shelving

Track shelving is the perfect choice if you want lots of shelves and need a system you can adjust easily as your storage needs change. The shelves sit on brackets that clip into slots in the wall-mounted tracks.

you will need

→ basic toolkit
→ shelf tracks
→ screws
→ wall plugs
→ shelf brackets
→ shelves

Putting up the tracks

❶ Mark the approximate positions for the tracks on the wall. Hold the first track up, mark the top screw hole position, and drill and plug the wall. Part-drive the screw so the track swings freely.

❷ Use a spirit level to check that the track is vertical, and mark the positions of the rest of the screw holes on the wall.

❸ Swing the track aside and drill holes at each of the marks. Insert wall plugs and drive in the fixing screws. Tighten the top screw as well.

❹ Hold the second track at its mark and set a spirit level on top of the two tracks to get them level. Mark the wall through the top screw hole, then repeat steps 2 and 3 to fix the second track to the wall.

Fitting the shelves

Fit the first pair of brackets into the tracks. Count slots down from the top to make sure they are at the same level.

Rest the first shelf on its brackets. Then add more brackets and shelves at the spacings you require.

If you want each shelf to fit flush with the wall, mark where it touches the tracks and make matching cut-outs to fit around them (see page 205).

(see page 205)

If the brackets have screw holes in them, use these to screw the shelves to the brackets. Hold each shelf on its brackets and mark the screw positions.

Take each shelf down and screw the brackets to it. Make sure the screws are not too long, or they will break through the top of the shelf.

Add a third or fourth track to extend the system. Fit long shelves to span all the tracks, and shorter ones to span adjacent track pairs.

Assembling flat-pack furniture

You can now buy all sorts of panel furniture in flat-pack form, from shelf units and wardrobes to kitchen cupboards. The manufacturer provides all the necessary fixing devices with each pack; all you have to do is put everything together.

Knock-down fixings

Here are four of the most common fixings used for flat-pack furniture

TIP

Read the instructions closely because many require holes to be drilled in precise positions relative to the edges of the panels.

you will need

→ basic tool kit
→ fixings pack
→ instruction leaflet

Two-part block joint

Two-part block joints are often used for simple box construction. One block is screwed to each panel, then a machine screw connects the blocks.

❶ Block with recessed nut

❷ Block with machine screw

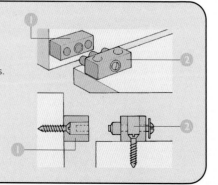

Cam fixing

Cam fixings consist of a cam stud screwed
into one component, and a locking cam set
in a hole drilled in the face of the other panel.
Once the panels are assembled, turning the
cam locks it on to the cam stud.

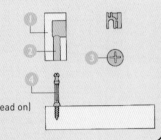

1 Hole for cam   **3** Cam (side and head on)

2 Hole for cam stud   **4** Cam stud

Screw socket

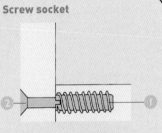

The screw socket consists of
a plastic or metal plug that is
inserted in the edge of one panel,
to receive a screw driven through
a hole drilled in the other panel.

1 Screw socket

2 Screw

Cross dowel

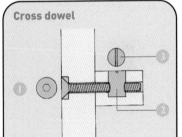

Cross dowels are used mainly
to link panels to rails. The steel
dowel fits in a hole in the rail,
and the screw passes through the
panel, into the rail and on into the
dowel, which can be aligned with
a screwdriver in its slot.

1 Hex-head machine screw

2 Cross dowel

3 Slot in cross dowel

Basic assembly techniques

Whenever you are assembling a piece of flat-pack furniture, start by unpacking the kit and finding the instruction sheet. Use this to check that all the parts listed have been included, especially the various fixing devices. Place these on a tray so they do not get lost, and count them type by type.

If any fixings are missing, return the unit to the store and ask for a complete replacement. Nothing is more frustrating than to get half-way through the assembly process before finding that you are short of a key component.

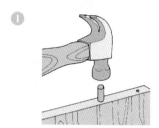

Many items of flat-pack furniture rely on using wooden dowels to form strong corner joints, plus a mechanical fixing to lock the panels together. Start by gluing dowels into all their holes.

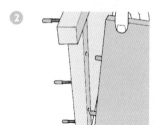

With screw sockets, tap sockets into the other pre-drilled holes in the edge with the dowels. Part-drive the screws into the holes in the other component, and bring the two together.

Tighten the screws into the sockets. Many of these fixings are assembled with a hex key, usually supplied with the fixings kit.

Basic boxes for shelving or drawers are usually stiffened and kept square with a hardboard back panel. Lay this on the side panels and attach it around the edges with panel pins.

Shelves may rest on plastic studs fitted in pre-drilled holes in the cabinet sides. Some units use special inserts that are tapped into pre-drilled holes in the undersides of the shelves.

The inserts lock on to screws driven into pre-drilled holes in the cabinet sides. Lower the shelf into place so the inserts engage on the screw heads.

TIP

As you assemble any piece of flat-pack furniture, use your try square to check that the structure is square before finally tightening screws and other fixings. If the basic unit is out of square, fitting shelves, doors and drawers will be difficult later on.

See pages 214–215 for cabinet assembly using cam fixings.

Assembling a flat-pack cabinet

A typical flat-pack cabinet consists of five panels forming the basic box, plus a door and possibly one or more shelves. A combination of glued wood dowels and cam fixings makes the basic box a sturdy structure.

Preparing the components

1 Lay out all the parts on the floor so you can identify them, and read the instructions. Start by fitting feet (if supplied) to the underside of the unit's base panel.

2 Screw cam studs into the outer pre-drilled holes in the base and top panels. Tighten them fully.

3 Tap a glued dowel into the other holes in the top and base panels, and wipe away any excess adhesive.

4 Fit a locking cam into each of the larger pre-drilled holes in the two side panels. Rotate the cam with a cross-point screwdriver so the arrow on its body points towards the edge of the panel.

Assembling the cabinet

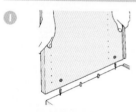

Apply adhesive to the dowels on the base panel, and fit the first side panel over the dowels and cam studs. Push it down as far as it will go.

Lock the two cams on to their studs by using a cross-point screwdriver to rotate each cam through 90°.

TIP

If the instructions require panels to
be glued together, assemble them
without adhesive to begin with so you
can check that they fit together properly.
It is difficult to make any adjustments
once the parts are glued up.

See page 216
for attaching hinges and
their mounting plates
to the cabinet.

Fit the back panel next. Run a bead of
glue into the grooves in the side and
base panels and slide the back panel
into place.

Apply adhesive to the groove in the top
panel, and lower it over the cam studs
and glued dowels in the sides. Tighten
the cams and fit their plastic covers.

Apply adhesive to the groove in the
second side panel. Lower it onto its cam
studs and glued dowels and engage the
edge of the back panel in the groove.
Tighten the cams.

Attach the hinges to the doors and hang
them by screwing their mounting plates
to the cabinet sides.

Fitting out a flat-pack cabinet

Once you have assembled the cabinet carcass, there will be several other jobs involved in fitting out the cabinet – adding door handles and hinges, for example, and assembling and fitting drawers.

you will need

→ screwdriver
→ drill
→ fixings pack
→ instruction leaflet

Fitting handles

❶ Hold the handle in place against the door and mark the positions of the fixing holes. Drill clearance holes through the door at each point to accept the screws.

❷ Push a screw through each hole in the door, offer up the handle and engage the screws. Tighten them up with a screwdriver.

Fitting hinges

Modern spring-loaded hinges fit into 35mm (1⅜in) diameter holes drilled in the inner face of the cabinet doors. Insert them and screw them on.

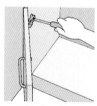

Loosen the rear screw on each hinge to get the door fitting flush with the cabinet. Adjust the front screw to get the door square to the cabinet.

Making and fitting drawers

Drawers also come in kit form nowadays. Start the assembly by fitting the drawer sides to the back.

Slide the drawer base into the grooves in the drawer sides and back. Fix it with short screws driven up from below.

Screw the retaining clips to the pre-drilled holes in the back of the drawer front. Then push the clips into the slots in the drawer sides.

Mark the positions for the screws securing the handle to the drawer front. Drill clearance holes at the marks and screw on the handle.

 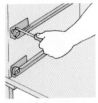

Screw the drawer runners to the pre-drilled holes in the cabinet sides. Check that left-hand and right-hand runners are on the correct sides.

Slide each drawer on to its runners and close the drawers. If any need adjusting to fit squarely, use the adjustment screws at the front of each drawer side.

A kitchen facelift

If your kitchen is beginning to look a bit worn and dated, the immediate reaction is to plan a complete replacement. However, simply changing the doors, the drawer fronts and the plinths and redecorating the room can give it a new lease of life.

Using tiles

1 You probably have tiled splashbacks above the worktops. Tiling over these with new tiles or mosaics is a quick and relatively inexpensive way of changing their looks. Modern tile adhesives will bond well to old tiles, so long as the existing surface is thoroughly clean and free from grease.

2 The only difficulty you may face lies in fitting tiles around obstacles such as switches and socket outlets. If you need to do this, turn off the power at the mains and unscrew each faceplate as you reach it.

3 Cut the tiles to match the cut-outs in the existing tiling, and fix them in place. Then buy extra-long faceplate fixing screws (available from DIY and electrical stores) and use these to reattach the faceplates so they cover the cut edges of the tiles. Restore the power when you have finished work.

4 If this sounds like too much trouble, at least consider giving the old tiles a thorough clean, and restoring discoloured grout to its former glory.

See page 135 for restoring discoloured grout.

Using paint

The cheapest (but not necessarily the quickest) way of changing the look of your kitchen is to paint the unit doors and drawer fronts. Remove each door or drawer front in turn, strip it of its hardware and wash it with household detergent to get rid of grease and dirt.

Rub the surface down with fine wet-and-dry abrasive paper, then wipe it with a cloth moistened with white spirit.

Treat melamine-faced doors and drawers with special melamine base coat, and follow this with melamine top coat or your choice of gloss or eggshell paint. You can paint varnished wood doors directly with gloss or eggshell paint, although you may need two coats to get good coverage. Complete the transformation by fitting new handles.

 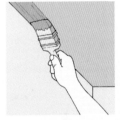

Use paint to freshen up wall and ceiling surfaces too. Wash them down well to remove grease, then apply one or two coats of kitchen and bathroom emulsion paint to provide a washable and hard-wearing finish.

Replacing doors and drawers

• Since the existing cabinet carcasses are probably in sound condition, cleaning them up and fitting new doors and drawer fronts will achieve a dramatic new look for the kitchen at quite modest expense.

• New doors and drawer fronts are widely advertised in home interest magazines, and are available in many different styles and finishes in a range of standard sizes.

• All you have to do is fit them. You can even reuse the existing hinges.

• You will need a special drill bit called an end mill bit to drill the shallow hinge recesses in the new doors.

• Most hinges require 35mm (1⅜in) diameter holes; be sure to check yours before you buy.

TIP

For an economy facelift, make your own replacement doors and drawers from off-the-shelf panels of veneered or plastic-coated chipboard. If available widths do not match your requirements exactly, trim doors down in width along the hinge edge and drawer fronts along the bottom edge. Disguise the cut edges with iron-on edge veneers if available, or with paint if not.

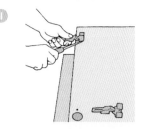

Unscrew the existing doors from their mounting plates. Undo the two screws holding each hinge to the door and prise them out of their recesses.

Use the old door as a template to mark the positions of the hinge recesses on the new doors. Drill out the holes to the same depth as the old ones, using an end mill bit.

Fit the existing hinges into the new recesses and secure them with the screws you removed in step 1. Fit new handles to each door (see page 216).

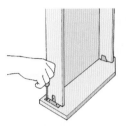

To replace drawer fronts, examine how the existing drawer boxes are attached to them. Undo the fixing screws and reattach the box to the new drawer front.

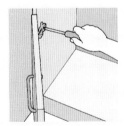

Offer up each new door and screw the hinge to the existing mounting plate in the cabinet. Adjust the screws (see page 216) to align the doors.

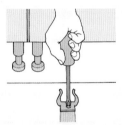

To replace old plinths, prise them off and use them as templates for cutting the new ones to height and length. Reuse existing clips or magnetic catches to mount the new plinths in place.

DIY storage solutions

However many (or few) DIY tasks you tackle, you need somewhere to store your tools and equipment so everything is easy to locate when you need it, and safely out of harm's way otherwise – especially if you have children in the family.

Tool storage

1 If you have any power tools without a carry case, you can buy empty cases in a range of sizes from DIY stores. Take your tools along and ask a member of staff if you can try them for size.

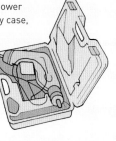

2 The best way of storing all but the largest hand tools (panel saws or long spirit levels, for example) is in a tool box with cantilevered or lift-out trays. You can carry it easily to wherever you are working, knowing that you have everything you need.

3 If you do your own wiring or plumbing work, you'll need specialized tools. Buy small tool cases for these, so that you can keep them separate from your ordinary DIY tools.

4 Tools such as saws and chisels come with blade guards to keep them sharp and safe when in storage. Hang saws that are too long for your tool box on wall hooks in the shed or garage, and keep chisels in their own storage boxes.

Workshop storage

1 If you have storage space in a garage or garden shed, use wall-mounted storage boxes and racks to hold small tools and other equipment.

2 Buy plastic storage boxes with inner compartments to keep things such as screws, nails, wall fixings and other hardware neat and tidy.

3 Buy sturdy metal shelving for the garage or shed in kit form, and bolt it together to create as much shelf space as you need.

Storage while you work

If you have a portable workbench, buy a clip-on tool tray that will stop tools from falling on the floor as you work.

Buy a tool trolley that you can load up in the garage with everything you need for the job, and then wheel it to where you are working.

If you are working off steps or a ladder, buy a leather or canvas tool belt so you can carry whatever tools and fixings you need with you.

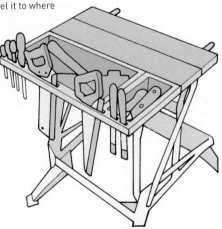

Plumbing: turning the water off

Water comes and water goes. So long as it behaves itself, there's no problem. But things do go wrong with household plumbing systems, and when they do, you need to act quickly if you are not to be flooded out.

Main stoptaps

The key control for your plumbing system is the main stoptap, which shuts off the supply of cold water from the water main in the street outside. Most houses have an indoor stoptap, usually located near the kitchen sink (1). Every property also has a second stoptap near the boundary of the property, buried up to 900mm (3ft) below ground in a vertical guard pipe and hidden beneath a small metal cover (2). If you have no indoor stoptap, this outdoor one is the only means you have of controlling the water supply. Get a plumber to install an indoor stoptap as soon as possible.

Check your indoor stoptap regularly to make sure it will turn freely; a jammed stoptap is no use in an emergency. Open it fully, then close it by about a quarter of a turn. Trickle penetrating oil down the tap spindle if it is stiff to turn.

Immediately above the indoor stoptap you will find a drain valve (3). This allows you to empty the pipe that runs up to the cold water storage tank.

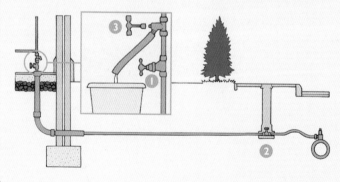

Other system controls

The diagram below shows a typical household water system, with a cold water storage tank (1) and a hot water cylinder (2). The smaller tank at loft level (3) keeps the heating system topped up, and is called the header or feed-and-expansion tank.

A control called a gate valve should be fitted on each outlet pipe from the cold water storage tank and the header tank. These allow you to stop water flowing to all the cold taps (4), to the hot water cylinder (5) and into the heating system (6) respectively. A drain valve at the base of the hot cylinder (7) permits you to empty this, and another by the boiler or a ground-floor radiator (8) lets you drain the heating system.

In a modern home, you will also find small isolating valves (9) on the hot and cold supply pipes to every water appliance. These allow taps and ballvalves to be isolated for repairs or replacement without the need to shut off and drain down large parts of the plumbing system.

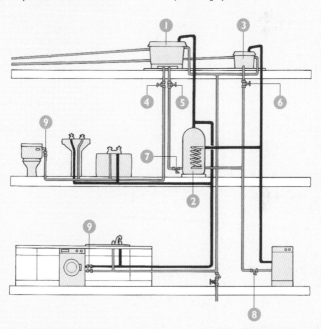

Changing a tap washer

Most taps contain a mechanism that raises and lowers a small piston inside the tap body to allow water to flow through it. The piston has a small rubber washer on the end, and if this perishes the tap will drip annoyingly. It costs a few pence to replace.

Turning off the water supply

❶ Isolating valve If there is an isolating valve on the pipe below the tap, use a screwdriver to turn the screw through 90°. Open the tap to check that the flow has stopped.

❷ Gate valve If there is no valve, go to the cold water storage tank and turn off the gate valves on the pipes running from its base. One feeds all the cold taps in the house (except the kitchen sink – see below). The other feeds the hot cylinder. Use trial and error to find out which is which. You can now open the dripping tap. A little water will flow, but you will not empty the hot cylinder because there is no pressure from the cold tank to force hot water out of it.

❸ Indoor stoptap If there are no gate valves, turn off the indoor stoptap and open all the cold taps to empty the cold water tank.

❹ Water tank If the stoptap is jammed, tie up the ballvalve float arm to a piece of wood laid across the top of the water tank. Then open the cold taps, as above.

• To work on the kitchen cold tap, turn off the main indoor stoptap.

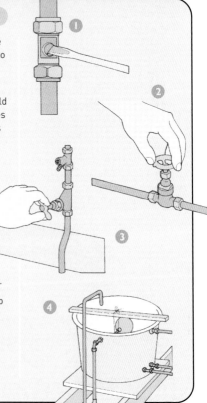

Replacing the tap washer

Examine the tap to see how the handle is fitted. Most have a disc on top to identify the tap. Prise the disc out.

 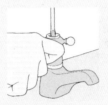

Undo the screw securing the tap handle and lift the handle off. If no screw is visible, simply pull the handle upwards.

Unscrew the tap body. Wrap it in a cloth to protect the chrome and use an adjustable spanner if it is stiff. This will expose the tap headgear.

Use an adjustable spanner again to undo the headgear nut. Brace the tap spout to stop the tap turning and damaging the connection below.

Lift out the headgear to reveal the piston and the washer on its end. Prise the washer off its stud, or release it by undoing the retaining nut with pliers.

 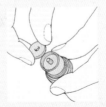

Fit a new washer on to the stud. Use a small washer on basin and sink taps, a large one on bath taps. Reverse the steps above to reassemble the tap.

Other cures for dripping taps

It is not only worn washers that make taps drip. Modern taps with ceramic disc mechanisms inside can start to drip as the discs wear. Rubber seals called O-rings can perish in mixer taps, and the seats inside tap bodies can get worn.

Ceramic disc taps

You can tell whether your taps have ceramic disc mechanisms inside by the way they work – off to full on in a quarter turn of the handle. This rotates the movable disc over the fixed one and aligns the holes in both discs, allowing water to flow. In theory the discs are maintenance-free, but in practice they can be scored by fine particles of grit in the water supply, and as a result they can start to leak. When this happens, you have to remove the ceramic disc cartridge and fit a replacement. Note that mixer taps have a left-handed and a right-handed cartridge, and you must fit the correct type for the tap to work.

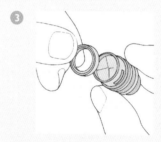

❶ To replace a cartridge, turn off the water supply (*page 226*), open the tap and remove the handle. Then unscrew the cartridge from the tap body, as for removing tap headgear (*page 227*).

❷ Lift out the old cartridge and take it with you to your plumbing supplier. He will be able to match it and supply the correct replacement. Screw it into the tap and replace the handle.

❸ Before replacing a suspect cartridge, examine the rubber seal on its end. If it is worn, you may be able to fit a replacement seal – far cheaper than buying a new cartridge.

TIP

Buy spare cartridges with new taps; there are many different types and they frequently go out of production before you need them.

Kitchen mixer taps

Drips from a kitchen mixer may be due to a worn tap washer (*see page 227*) or ceramic disc cartridge. Replace these as necessary. If water seeps from the point where the swivelling spout meets the tap body, the cause is probably perished rubber O-rings on the spout.

❶ Look for a small grub screw locking the spout to the tap, often located at the back of the spout. Undo it with an offset screwdriver and lift the spout off.

❷ If there is no grub screw, align the spout with the tap body and pull it upwards sharply to remove it.

❸ Prise the old O-rings off the end of the spout with a small screwdriver. Fit replacements after coating them with silicone grease (from your plumbing supplier), and replace the spout.

Fixing a worn seat

Inside a conventional tap, the washer closes against the water inlet. Over time, this surface can become scratched and pitted, allowing water to seep past the washer when the tap is turned off. You can fix the problem in two ways.

❶ Turn off the water supply, and unscrew and remove the tap headgear (*see page 227*). Prise out the piston and washer (called the jumper unit).

❷ Buy a seat repair kit containing a replacement jumper unit plus a special nylon seat liner. Press the liner into the tap seat, fit the new jumper unit into the tap headgear and reassemble the tap.

❸ Buy a tap re-seating tool, available from plumbing suppliers. Screw it into the tap body, adjust the cutter so it touches the seat and turn the handle to grind the metal smooth.

Clearing a blocked waste pipe

Plastic waste pipes carry water away from baths, basins, bidets, shower trays and kitchen sinks. Bathroom waste pipes can become blocked by scum, hair and shaving foam. Kitchen waste pipes get blocked mainly by solidified fat and food debris.

Using a plunger

The first method to use to clear a blocked waste pipe is a plunger. This creates pressure in the waste pipe and, with luck, forces the blockage out.

❶ Block the overflow from the appliance with a wet cloth. Place the plunger cup over the outlet and plunge it up and down several times.

❷ If this fails, try a hand-operated hydraulic pump. Fill it with water from the tap, then place it over the outlet and pump the handle up and down.

Using chemicals

There are several chemical products on the market that claim to clear blocked waste pipes. Sometimes they work (it depends on what is blocking the pipe), but if they do not, you are left with an appliance full of noxious chemical and no obvious way of getting rid of it. The best advice is not to use them. And stop pouring liquid fat down the sink!

Using a plughole snake

Another tool that is very useful for clearing blocked waste pipes is the plughole snake.

This contains a coil of spring wire (like curtain wire, but without the plastic coating), which you insert through the outlet grille of the appliance.

Turning the top handle pushes the flexible wire around the trap and into the waste pipe to move the blockage.

If plungers and pumps fail to shift the blockage, you will have to disconnect the trap under the appliance from the waste pipe so you can clear it directly.

Dismantling the pipework

Put the plug in and place a bucket beneath the trap. Undo the nut connecting the trap to the waste outlet.

Next, undo the nut connecting the other end of the trap to the waste pipe. Use an adjustable wrench if it is stiff.

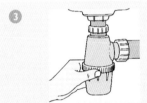

Some appliances have a one-piece bottle trap. Unscrew the base of the trap to gain access to its insides.

Fill a washing-up bowl with household detergent and use an old toothbrush to scrub out the trap. Reconnect the trap and waste pipe, and pull out the plug.

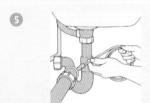

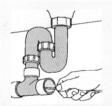

If the trap is clear and the blockage persists, disconnect the trap from the pipe and feed in a flexible drain snake or a straightened wire coat-hanger.

If the trap has a rodding eye, unscrew this and feed in the drain snake or coat-hanger wire. Flush it through with hot soapy water once clear.

Fixing faulty ballvalves

The flow of water into a cold water storage tank or a WC cistern is controlled automatically by a float-operated valve, commonly known as a ballvalve. If it stops working properly, either the tank overflows or it doesn't refill as it empties.

Adjusting the water level

Water tanks and cisterns should fill automatically to about 25mm (1in) below the level of the overflow pipe. If the level is too high, water will overflow. If the level in a WC cistern is too low, the WC may not flush properly.

1 In a cold water storage tank, bend the float arm up or down slightly to alter the water level.

2 If the float is attached to a vertical section of the float arm, loosen the locking screw and slide the float up or down to alter the water level.

3 If the float is sitting low in the water, it may have developed a puncture. Remove it, drill holes in it to let the water out and re-fit it. Tie a small plastic bag over it and secure it with a wire tie. Buy and fit a new float as soon as possible.

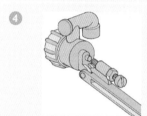

4 Plastic ballvalves have an adjustment mechanism. Loosen the locknut and turn the screw in to lower the water level, out to raise it. Retighten the locknut.

TIP

While fixing the overflow problem, check the joints on the overflow pipe are secure. Either solvent-weld or stick them with duct tape.

Repairing a piston valve

Brass Portsmouth pattern valves contain a small piston with a rubber washer on one end. If the washer perishes, the valve will not shut off properly and the tank will overflow with a persistent and annoying drip.

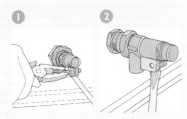

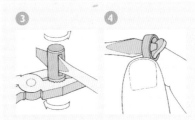

❶ Turn off the water supply to the valve. Unscrew the end cap from the valve body and pull out the metal split pin that attaches the float arm to the piston assembly.

❷ Insert the tip of a screwdriver blade in the slot beneath the valve body and lever the piston out.

❸ Grip the piston end cap with pliers and insert the screwdriver tip in the slot. Turn it to separate the two parts of the piston.

❹ Poke the old washer out of the piston end cap and fit a replacement of the same size. Reassemble the piston and valve, and restore the water supply.

Repairing a diaphragm valve

More modern ballvalves have a larger body with an overhead water outlet, and contain a rubber diaphragm rather than a small washer. Replacing a worn diaphragm is even easier than replacing the washer on a Portsmouth valve.

❶ Turn off the water supply to the valve. Pull out the split pin attaching the float arm and set both aside. Unscrew the valve end cap using slip-joint pliers or an adjustable wrench.

❷ Lift off the cap and plunger and prise out the old diaphragm. Fit a same-size replacement with the raised outer circle on the outside, reassemble the valve and restore the water supply.

Fixing WC flush problems

The usual reason why a WC cistern will not flush is because a cheap component called a flap inside the siphon mechanism has failed. Replacing it can be a fiddly job unless you are lucky enough to have a two-part siphon unit.

What's inside the cistern

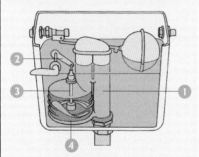

The heart of a WC's flush mechanism is the U-shaped siphon unit attached to the cistern outlet. When you press the flush lever, the lift rod raises the piston inside the open end of the siphon unit, forcing water up and over the U-bend to start the siphon action.

The piston is an open frame, and a flexible plastic flap sits on top of it, held down by the weight of water. After the siphon action has started, the piston drops back down and the flap rises to allow water to fill the siphon chamber again, ready for the next flush.

Repeated use eventually causes the flap to tear, preventing the piston from lifting water over the U-bend. That is usually why the WC will not flush.

❶ Siphon unit

❷ Lift rod

❸ Piston

❹ Flap

Two-part siphons

If your WC cistern is fitted with a two-part siphon unit, you can simply disconnect the part containing the piston and flap. Undo the knurled nut that connects the siphon chamber to the vertical pipe leading to the cistern outlet, and lift the chamber out. Some siphon units are in three parts, as shown here.

Removing the cistern

Turn off the water supply to the cistern, flush it and bail out as much water as possible. Be ready to mop up some water spillage as you disconnect the cistern.

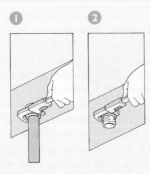

1 If your WC has a separate flush pipe linking pan and cistern, disconnect it from the cistern outlet.

2 Then undo the nut that connects the siphon unit to the outlet hole in the base of the cistern.

3 If the WC is close-coupled, undo the nuts holding the cistern to the pan, and disconnect the supply and overflow pipes. Undo the screws holding the cistern to the wall and lift it off the pan.

4 Turn the close-coupled cistern upside-down and unscrew the nut holding the siphon unit to the base of the cistern as before.

Replacing the flap

Disconnect the wire link between the lift rod and the piston, and lift the siphon unit out of the cistern.

Slide the piston out of the base of the siphon unit. Remove the spring and the retaining washer from the shaft to free the old flap.

Buy a same-size replacement flap, fit it over the piston shaft, and replace the washer and spring. Reattach the siphon unit to the cistern and reassemble everything in reverse order.

Fixing other WC problems

Faulty flushing is just one of the problems that can affect your WC. Others include blockages in the trap, leaks from the trap connection at the back and even a broken toilet seat. Here's how to fix things.

Clearing blockages

A blocked WC is one of the less pleasant problems you may have to deal with. It may be caused by over-zealous use of toilet paper, by attempts to flush away unsuitable things like disposable nappies, or by inquisitive toddlers sending soft toys on potholing expeditions. Whatever the cause, it needs prompt action.

Put on rubber gloves and fish out any obvious blockage. Then use a larger version of the sink plunger (which you can hire) or a multi-stranded household mop to attempt to shift the blockage. Pump it up and down a few times. If the blockage clears, the pan will empty with a gurgling sound. Flush away the remains of the blockage with a bucketful of hot soapy water.

If a plunger does not work, hire a flexible drain auger. Pass the flexible spring wire into the pan and around the trap, then rotate the handle to drive the end of the auger into the blockage. Flush the trap out with soapy water. Wash and disinfect the auger before you return it to the hire shop.

Leaking traps

You may discover a leak from the rear of the pan, where the trap is connected into the soil pipe. In most houses, they will be joined by a flexible plastic connector. This may have perished over time and need replacing.

If you have a separate cistern, disconnect the flush pipe from the pan. If the cistern is close-coupled, empty it and disconnect the supply and overflow pipes. Then unscrew the cistern from the wall and the pan from the floor.

❶ Pull the pan carefully away from the soil pipe until the outlet on the back of the pan is free.

❷ Pull the old pan connector off, clean the spigot on the pan and the end of the soil pipe, and fit a new connector on the pan outlet.

❸ Push the pan carefully back into place so the connector fits snugly over the end of the soil pipe. Then screw it to the floor and reconnect the cistern.

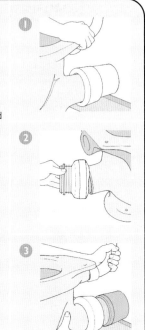

Replacing the seat

The most common cause of broken toilet seats or lids is people standing on them. The weight will fracture them between the supports that rest on the lip of the pan.

❶ Unscrew the nuts fixing the old seat and lid to the rear of the pan. Clean around the fixing holes. Then attach the hinge fittings to the replacement seat.

❷ Position the new seat with its bolts through the fixing holes. Fit washers above and below the pan. Check that the seat sits squarely on the pan, and do up the fixing nuts as tightly as possible.

Fixing a leaky overflow pipe

If your cistern has a bottom-entry overflow pipe, a leak may develop at the connection point. What happens is that the inner sealing washer between the overflow standpipe and the base of the cistern perishes. To replace it, empty the cistern, disconnect the overflow pipe and undo the backnut securing the standpipe. Lift it out, replace the washer and reassemble everything in the reverse order.

Fixing leaks and burst pipes

Plumbing and heating pipework sometimes develops a leak, either from the pipe itself or at a fitting. If you have uninsulated pipes in cold places, such as in lofts or under-floor voids, they may freeze in cold weather and burst when they thaw out.

Fixing leaking joints

Leaks commonly develop at brass compression joints – the type you assemble with a spanner – if the nuts are over-tightened. This deforms the soft ring (olive) inside the fitting.

❶ Undo the leaking end of the joint, push the capnut away from the olive and slip the pipe end out of the fitting. Use a hacksaw to cut off the olive.

❷ Clean the end of the pipe with wire wool or fine glasspaper. Then slip a new olive on to the end of the pipe.

❸ Reassemble the joint and hand-tighten the capnut on to the body of the fitting. Then give it one complete turn with a spanner. Check that the joint is watertight. If it still weeps, give the nut a further quarter turn.

Repairing a leaking soldered joint is more difficult for the amateur to fix. The best solution is to drain the pipework, cut out the fitting with a hacksaw and replace it with a push-fit connector (*see page 239*).

Fixing a leaking pipe

Copper pipe sometimes develops tiny pinhole leaks, caused by impurities in the pipe corroding the pipe wall. The resulting leak is usually small in volume, but eventually a large damp patch will appear in the vicinity of the leak – usually on a ceiling.

A frozen pipe will often split as the ice inside expands. When it thaws, it will leak, and the bigger the split, the bigger the mess. Prompt action is needed to deal with the situation. Start by turning off the water supply and draining the affected pipe (*see pages 224–226*).

The solution to leaking and burst pipes is the same. Make an immediate emergency repair if you can, then replace the damaged pipe with a new piece as soon as possible.

Emergency repairs

Be prepared for disaster by keeping a two-part pipe repair clamp in your toolkit. Fit one half behind the pipe, with the rubber gasket over the split, and screw the other half to it.

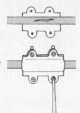

If you do not have a clamp, improvise with garden hose and stiff garden wire. Split the hose length-ways, fit it around the pipe and tie it on with wire twists, tightened with pliers.

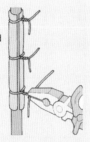

TIP

You can use ordinary copper pipe to make the repair, but you will have to buy a 2m (6ft) length and cut off what you want. A pipe repair kit will be cheaper, and it is a good idea to keep one in your plumbing toolkit.

Permanent repairs

Use a pipe slice or a hacksaw to cut out the section containing the pinhole or split. Clean the pipe ends with wire wool or fine glasspaper.

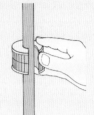

Buy two plastic push-fit connectors and a short piece of corrugated copper pipe (often sold together as a pipe repair kit). Push a fitting on to each cut end of the pipe.

Bend the corrugated pipe slightly so you can push the plain ends into the fittings. Then pull each end of the pipe out slightly to lock it into its fitting.

239

Fixing radiator problems

Central heating radiators are just hollow steel panels (unless they are posh designer types). They corrode inside, producing gas that reduces the radiator's heat output, and eventually they can develop pinhole leaks along the seams.

Bleeding a radiator

If a radiator feels cold at the top when the heating is on, it probably has gas or air in it. You can remove this by opening the air vent in one of the radiator's top corners. This is usually a small square plug screwed into a threaded fitting, and it is opened with a special key (as shown). Some new radiators have a vent that you undo with a flat-tip screwdriver to bleed the system.

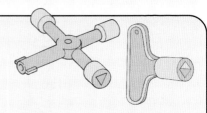

❶ Open the air vent with the key. Hold a pad of kitchen roll underneath to catch any drips as the air is expelled. Grip the key with pliers for extra leverage if the vent plug is stiff to turn.

Fixing a leaky connection

Leaks can develop where the radiator valve is connected to the radiator inlet or outlet. Cure the problem by undoing and resealing the joint. You will need a large shallow container to collect the contents of the radiator, and dust sheets.

❶ Undo the nut on the side of the valve with a spanner. Brace the valve against the skirting board with another spanner so you do not bend the pipe below.

❷ Wind some plumber's PTFE sealing tape around the threaded section of the valve outlet. Then reconnect the nut to it and tighten it with a spanner.

Replacing a radiator

If a radiator develops a leak, you have little choice but to replace it with a new one of the same size. You may be able to fix the leak temporarily with two-part epoxy repair putty. Otherwise shut off the radiator by closing both valves (1), and undo the valve connectors (*see page 240*) so you can drain the affected radiator of water.

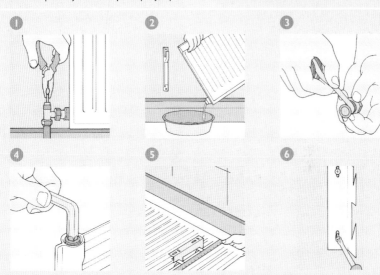

❷ Disconnect the radiator valves, lift the radiator off its brackets and drain its contents into buckets.

❸ Wrap PTFE tape around the threads of the new inlet and outlet connectors, the air vent and the blanking plug for the remaining top corner of the replacement radiator.

❹ Use a radiator spanner to screw all these components into their respective sockets on the radiator.

❺ Check whether the new radiator will fit on the existing brackets. If it will, hang it ready for reconnection. If it will not, measure up the new bracket positions and mark these on the wall.

❻ Screw the brackets to the wall at the marks, lift the new radiator on to them and reconnect the valves to the valve connectors. Open both radiator valves to refill the new radiator, and check for any leaks.

Insulating tanks and pipes

If your cold water storage tank and the central heating system's feed-and-expansion tank are in the loft, they are at risk of freezing in winter weather. So is any exposed pipework in the loft or in ventilated under-floor voids. They all need insulating.

Insulating tanks

You can buy ready-made insulating jackets for storage and feed-and-expansion tanks. They consist of sections of glassfibre insulation enclosed in plastic, and come complete with string or tape ties.

❶ Unroll the wrap-around section and shake it to fluff up the insulation. Place it around the tank and tie it in place.

❷ Place the top panel on the tank and mark where the vent pipe passes through the tank lid. Make a cut in the panel up to the mark.

❸ Fit the top panel around the vent pipe and tuck the edges inside the wrap-around section.

❹ Use PVC tape to seal the cut in the top panel. Stick strips across the cut first, then add a longer piece along it.

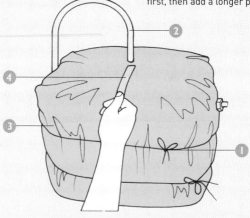

Insulating pipework

The best insulating material for pipes is foam plastic pipe lagging. This is sold in sizes to fit different pipe diameters. They are pre-slit along their length so you can fit them around the pipes. Use the new thick-wall types of lagging for extra insulation.

 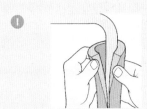

Open up the slit with your thumb and fit the insulation around the pipe. Press the slit closed. Butt lengths together.

Use a hacksaw or a serrated bread knife to cut the insulation to length, and to make 45° cuts so you can fit it neatly at elbow and tee joints.

 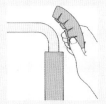

If the pipe has a bend rather than a sharp elbow, cut small wedges out of the split edge of the insulation so you can fit it around the curve.

 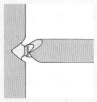

At tee joints, make 45° cuts in both sections of the insulation and fit them together neatly.

Use PVC tape or proprietary plastic clips (sold with the insulation) to hold joints and seams together.

Electrics: how the system works

Unless you plan to do your own home wiring work, what you really need to know about your home wiring system is how it works, and what to do when something goes wrong and the lights go out.

System controls

The heart of your electrical system is what used to be called the fusebox, but is now properly known as the consumer unit. This is a wall-mounted plastic or metal enclosure that contains the system's main on/off switch, and distributes electricity to the various light and power circuits in the house.

In an older system, each circuit will be protected by a fuse to stop it being overloaded. This will be either a wire fuse fitted between the terminals of the fuseholder, or an enclosed cartridge fuse like the ones used in UK plugs. The fuse is rated according to the amount of current the circuit uses – for example, 5 amps for light circuits, 15 amps for the circuit to the immersion heater, 30 amps for power circuits supplying socket outlets, and 45 amps for the cooker circuit.

In a modern system, miniature circuit breakers (MCBs) replace the fuses. These are sensitive switches that trip off if an overload or other fault occurs. They can also be switched off to isolate a circuit for repairs.

Modern systems may include a residual current device (RCD), which protects users from the risks of electric shock. It usually controls the power circuits.

The fusebox or consumer unit is connected to the electricity meter by two thick cables. Two more cables (known as 'tails') link the meter to the service head, where the incoming supply cable is connected.

Safety

Working with electrics can be dangerous, so if you are in any doubt, then contact a qualified professional. When working with electricity, *always* turn off the power supply at the mains.

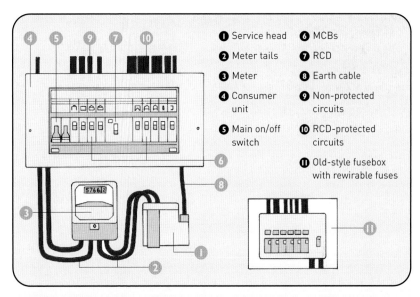

1 Service head
2 Meter tails
3 Meter
4 Consumer unit
5 Main on/off switch
6 MCBs
7 RCD
8 Earth cable
9 Non-protected circuits
10 RCD-protected circuits
11 Old-style fusebox with rewirable fuses

Loop-in lighting circuits

Most modern homes have loop-in lighting circuits.

The circuit cable runs into each ceiling rose or light fitting, then on to the next one, and the switch cable is connected directly into the rose or fitting.

You can tell if you have loop-in wiring by undoing the screw-on cover of a ceiling rose. If more than one cable is present, you have a loop-in wiring system.

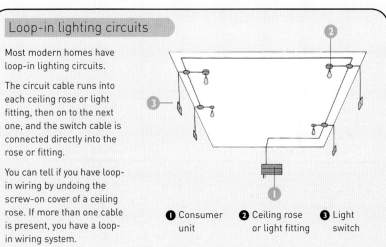

1 Consumer unit
2 Ceiling rose or light fitting
3 Light switch

Junction-box lighting circuits

In older homes, the lighting circuit cable runs into and out of a series of round junction boxes. At each box, separate cables connect it to a nearby light fitting and to its switch. If you have this type of wiring, there will be only one cable present at a ceiling rose or light fitting.

❶ Consumer unit   **❷** Junction box   **❸** Ceiling rose or light fitting   **❹** light switch

Light circuits

Your house will probably have two light circuits – one for upstairs and one for downstairs.

Each will start at a 5-amp fuseholder or MCB in the fusebox or consumer unit. The cable runs from one light position to the next, and the circuit finishes at the most remote one.

Each circuit supplies a maximum load of about 1,200 watts. In practice, each circuit supplies up to eight lighting points, to allow for the use of high-wattage light bulbs without overloading the circuit.

Power circuits

Your house will also have several power circuits. At least two (and possibly more) will supply socket outlets for portable appliances.

There will also be single circuits to power-hungry appliances such as the cooker, the immersion heater and an electric shower if one is installed. Each will start at a fuse or MCB, rated to match the current consumption of the circuit.

Circuits to socket outlets

Most homes have so-called ring-main circuits supplying socket outlets.

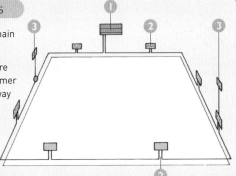

❶ Both ends of the circuit cable are connected to the fusebox or consumer unit so electricity can flow either way around the ring, increasing its current-carrying capacity. The circuit is protected by a 30-amp fuse or MCB.

❷ The cable runs into and out of each socket outlet.

❸ Extra outlets can be connected to the ring by a spur cable wired into a socket on the ring or into a junction box on the circuit cable.

Circuits to appliances

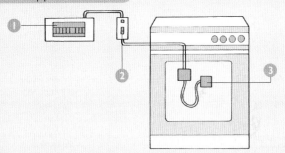

The circuit cable runs from the fuse or MCB in the fusebox or consumer unit (1) to a double-pole isolating switch (2), and then on to the appliance itself (3).

The circuits use thick, heavy-duty cables to carry the high current demand.

Tracing electrical faults

When an electrical fault develops, something stops working. Often the reason is quite easy to find, and putting the problem right need not involve any major electrical work. This checklist will help you find faults and tell you when to call an electrician.

If a light goes out...

• Check whether the light bulb has failed. Turn off the light switch and fit a replacement bulb of the correct type and wattage. Switch on and test.

• Switch on other lights on the same circuit. If none works, the circuit fuse or MCB has cut off the supply. It will do this if a short circuit has occurred due to a loose connection or a broken wire. This is most likely to happen in the pendant flex attached to a ceiling rose. It will also happen if you overload the circuit with too many high-wattage light bulbs – the maximum wattage a light circuit can supply is about 1200 watts. Reconnect or replace the flex (*page 254*), and fit lower-wattage light bulbs. Then replace the circuit fuse or reset the MCB (*pages 251–252*).

• With table and standard lamps, check the plug fuse (*page 250*), the flex connections in the plug and light fitting, and the flex itself (*page 253*). Fit a new fuse and make any necessary repairs.

If an appliance stops working...

• Unplug it and plug another appliance in at the same socket outlet. If this works, the fault is in the first appliance. Check its plug fuse and replace it if necessary. Make sure the flex connections in the plug are secure. If you can, check the flex connections to the appliance. Replace the flex if it is damaged in any way.

• If the second appliance does not work at the original socket outlet, the circuit fuse or MCB may have cut off the supply. Replace the fuse or reset the MCB (*pages 251–252*).

• If the appliance feels hot or you smell burning, unplug it and have it checked by a service engineer.

If a whole circuit is dead...

• Switch off all the lights and unplug all the appliances on the affected circuit. Check whether the circuit fuse or MCB has cut off the supply. Replace the fuse or reset the MCB (*pages 251–252*).

• Switch lights on and plug appliances in one by one. If one light or appliance causes the circuit fuse to blow again, or the MCB trips off, isolate the offender for testing and repair. Restore the circuit power supply as above so other lights or appliances on the circuit work.

• If the fuse fails or the MCB trips off as soon as you restore the power, there is a fault somewhere on the circuit wiring. You can check whether connections inside wiring accessories (switches, socket outlets, etc) are faulty by unscrewing their faceplates and tightening up all the terminal screws. Make sure the power is turned off before you do this. Alternatively, call in an electrician to trace the fault.

• Check whether you are overloading a power circuit. A ring-main circuit can supply up to about 3000 watts (3 kilowatts, or kW for short). Plugging in several high-wattage appliances (mainly those with heating elements) may exceed this limit, causing an overload that will blow the circuit fuse or trip its MCB. Unplug the offenders.

If everything is dead...

• Suspect a power cut and call neighbours to see if they have lost power too. Report a local power failure to your supply company's 24-hour emergency telephone number, usually listed under 'Electricity' in your telephone directory. The company will confirm if there is a local fault, and should be able to tell you when power will be restored.

• If only your house is affected, check whether your whole system is protected by a residual current device (RCD) in the consumer unit. If it is and the RCD has tripped off, switch it back on. Whole-system RCDs are no longer used in new houses, but some earlier wiring installations have an RCD in place of the main on/off switch.

• If this RCD cannot be reset, the fault that caused it to trip off is still present. Use the appliance and circuit checks described earlier to track it down. Alternatively, call an electrician. If this RCD trips off regularly for no apparent reason and can be immediately reset (a fault known as nuisance tripping), contact your supply company.

• If you do not have a whole-house RCD, the fault lies in your incoming supply. Call the 24-hour emergency number and ask for an engineer to come and repair the fault.

Replacing fuses

Fuses protect house circuits and individual appliances from electrical faults, such as short circuits or overloading, melting and cutting off the supply if one occurs. You need to know how to replace or repair them when they 'blow', so you can get the power back on quickly.

Replacing a plug fuse

In the UK, plugs with rectangular pins contain a small cartridge fuse. This will blow if a fault develops inside the plug – a short circuit, for example, caused by a bare wire coming away from its terminal and touching another wire or terminal. It will also blow if such a fault develops inside the appliance or flex.

❶ If you suspect that a plug fuse has blown, unscrew the plug top and prise the fuse from its retaining clips with a small screwdriver.

Factory-fitted plugs (and plug-in adapters) cannot be opened in this way. The fuse is fitted in a removable holder, which you have to prise open to release the fuse.

❷ Test whether the fuse has blown by using a continuity tester. If you do not have one, fit the fuse in the plug of a working appliance and test it that way.

❸ Replace a blown fuse with a new one of the correct rating. Use a 3-amp fuse for lights and small appliances rated at less than 700 watts, and a 13-amp fuse for more powerful appliances.

❹ Some appliances are wired directly into a wall-mounted fused connection unit (FCU). These contain a plug fuse in a concealed holder. Switch the FCU off and prise open the holder with a screwdriver to release the fuse.

❹

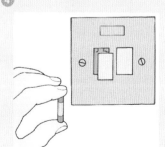

Replacing circuit fuses

Be prepared

If you have wired fuse holders in your consumer unit, make sure you have a supply of spare fuse wire in three ratings – 5, 15 and 30 amps.

If you have cartridge fuses, keep spare cartridges in each rating your fusebox requires. Each rating is colour-coded for ease of identification: white = 5 amps; blue = 15 amps; yellow = 20 amps; red = 30 amps; green = 45 amps.

TIP

Buy three spare fuse holders (labelled to match these ratings) and wire each with the correct fuse wire. Keep them by the fusebox so you can slot the appropriate one in when a fuse blows, and repair the blown one at your leisure.

Cartridge fuses

Some cartridge fuse holders carry the fuse in two spring clips. Prise the old fuse out and clip in the replacement.

Others have the fuse enclosed by the fuseholder pins. Open the holder, fit the new fuse and reassemble it.

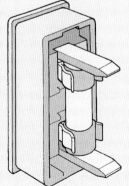
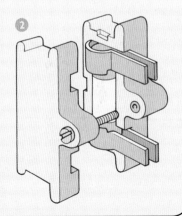

Rewirable fuses

1 Turn the power off and remove the affected fuse holder.

2 Undo the terminal screws.

3 Remove the remains of the old fuse wire.

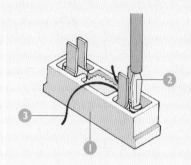

1 Connect new wire of the correct rating to one terminal.

2 Lay it across the centre of the fuse holder and attach it securely to the other terminal.

3 Snip off the excess wire.

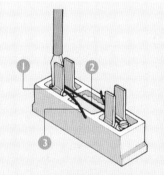

1 With some fuse holders, you need to thread the wire through a ceramic tube between the terminals.

2 Replace the fuseholder when you have rewired it and turn the power on.

Resetting an MCB or RCD

Some MCBs have a push button, others an on/off switch. To reset the MCB, either push the button in or flick the switch to 'on'. An RCD will have an on/off switch.

Working with flex

Flex (short for flexible cord) connects portable appliances to their plugs, and pendant lampholders to their ceiling roses. You may need to test it for electrical continuity, replace it or simply extend it if it is not long enough for your needs.

Testing flex

Flex flexes. That is why it is called flex. But it also gets yanked, tripped over, trodden on and, in the case of pendant lampholders, swung backwards and forwards in the breeze. This can cause individual wires inside (called cores) to wear and break. If this happens, current will not flow through it, but you cannot see the problem because it is hidden by the outer sheath of the flex. The only way of finding the fault is with a continuity tester, a battery-powered device that sends a small current through whatever it is testing.

• Disconnect the flex you want to test from its terminals at both ends.

• Press the probes of the tester to each end of each core in turn. If the tester light comes on, there is electrical continuity through that core.

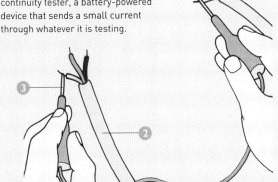

❶ Cores

❷ Outer sheath

❸ Continuity tester

Replacing flex

If you need to replace a flex, it must be the right type for the job and have the correct current rating.

• Use flat two-core flex for wiring small double-insulated appliances, and for light fittings with no metallic parts.

• Use round two-core flex for wiring up plastic pendant lampholders, and for small double-insulated appliances if you prefer it to flat flex.

• Use round three-core flex for all lights and appliances that need earthing.

• Use unkinkable flex on portable appliances such as irons, where the flex has to withstand movement and wear.

• Use curly flex where you want it to stretch and contract in use.

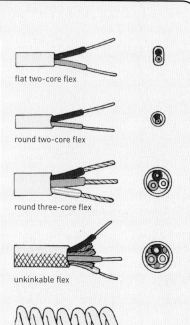

flat two-core flex

round two-core flex

round three-core flex

unkinkable flex

curly flex

Current ratings

Flex is rated by the cross-sectional area of its conductors in sq mm. Match the size you use to the appliance wattage.

• $0.5mm^2$ – max 700 watts

• $0.75mm^2$ – max 1,300 watts

• $1.0mm^2$ – max 2,300 watts

• $1.25mm^2$ – max 2,900 watts

• $1.5mm^2$ – max 3,600 watts

Extending flex safely

If you need to lengthen an appliance flex so it will reach a socket outlet, use a one-piece flex connector. Disconnect the flex from its plug (or cut off a factory-fitted plug and prepare the cores for wiring to the connector).

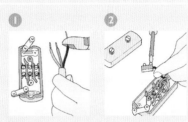 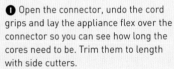 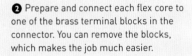 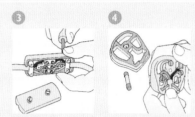

❶ Open the connector, undo the cord grips and lay the appliance flex over the connector so you can see how long the cores need to be. Trim them to length with side cutters.

❷ Prepare and connect each flex core to one of the brass terminal blocks in the connector. You can remove the blocks, which makes the job much easier.

❸ Connect the cores of the new flex to the terminal blocks so like-coloured cores share the same block. Then fit and screw down the two cord grips and screw on the cover.

❹ Prepare the cores at the other end of the new flex and connect them to the plug. Anchor the sheath in the cord grip, fit the fuse and close the plug.

Replacing pendant flex

Cut the new flex to length and prepare the cores for connection by stripping off the sheath and the core insulation.

❶ Thread the flex through the hole in the lampholder cover and connect its cores to the two terminals. Loop the cores around the two support lugs and screw on the cover.

❷ Turn the power to the lighting circuit off. Thread the other end of the flex through the ceiling rose cover and connect its cores to the two outer terminals of the rose. Hook the cores over the support lugs and screw on the cover.

Updating wiring accessories

If you are redecorating a room, among features you might want to change are the light switches, socket outlets and other wiring accessories. If they are boring white plastic, you can fit new coloured, metallic or wooden ones in a variety of finishes.

Replacing a light switch

Turn off the power supply to the lighting circuit and undo the screws securing the switch to its wall box. Ease the faceplate away from the wall.

 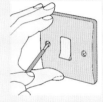

If the faceplate is plastic and the wall box is metal, the cable earth core will be wired to the earth terminal in the box. Release the red and black cores.

 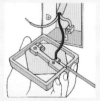

Reconnect the red and black cores to the terminals of the new switch faceplate, and screw it to the wall box.

If the faceplate is metal, remove the bare earth from some scrap cable, cover it with green-and-yellow PVC sleeving and use it to connect the switch earth terminal to the box.

Fitting a dimmer switch

You can replace an ordinary light switch with a dimmer switch to enable you to control the brightness of the room's lighting. When choosing one, check the wattage of the lights it will control, as most have a defined wattage range. Check the depth of the existing switch wall box too. This may be only 16mm (⅝in) deep, and some dimmers need a deeper box to accommodate the dimmer electronics. If your box is only a shallow one, look for a dimmer designed to fit this type of box.

❶ To fit a dimmer, turn off the power supply to the lighting circuit. Disconnect the existing switch cable and reconnect it to the dimmer terminals.

❷ Follow the instructions supplied with the dimmer.

Replacing a socket outlet

❶ Turn off the power to the socket outlet circuit and undo the screws securing the faceplate to its wall box.

❷ Ease the faceplate away from the wall and inspect the existing wiring.

❸ If only one circuit cable is present, undo the terminal screws and discard the old faceplate.

❹ Reconnect the red cable core to the live (L) terminal on the new faceplate, the black core to neutral (N) and the earth core to the earth terminal.

❺ If the earth core is bare, cover it with green-and-yellow PVC sleeving.

❻ If two cables are present, release them as before and reconnect them so matched pairs of coloured cores go to each terminal.

❼ Make sure both cores are securely held by the terminal screws.

❽ Fold the circuit cables carefully back into the mounting box, press the new faceplate into position and replace the fixing screws.

❾ Restore the power supply.

OUTDOORS

Repairing brickwork

If your house has brick walls or you have brick features in the garden, you'll know that the weather can be hard on them. Surfaces become dirty and stained, and rainwater and frost can damage both the bricks and the pointing (mortar joints).

Cleaning masonry

• If your brickwork is merely a bit grubby, you can work wonders by hosing it down and scrubbing it with a stiff-bristled brush. Start at the top of the wall and work your way down.

• For more stubborn stains, hire or buy a power washer. Most come with a 10m (30ft) hose, so you can use it from a ladder with the machine on the ground. Make sure the windows are shut.

• If your brickwork has efflorescence – a white powdery deposit on the surface – brush it off dry. Once the deposits stop recurring, consider treating the wall with a clear masonry sealer to keep damp out.

• Clean stray paint splashes from brickwork around windows and doors with chemical paint stripper. Dab it on, leave it for an hour to soften the paint, then scrub and rinse off the residue.

❶ Trigger-operated lance

❷ Power washer

❸ Cleaning solution

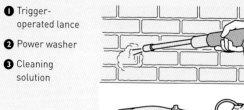

Repointing brickwork

If the mortar joints between the bricks are beginning to crumble and fall out, they need repointing. For small areas, buy a bag of dry ready-mixed mortar and mix up only as much as you need.

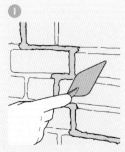

❶ Chop out the loose mortar with a slim cold chisel and a club hammer, and brush out all the loose material. Brush some diluted PVA building adhesive along the joint to help the mortar stick.

❷ Mix up the mortar and place it on a board or hawk. Scoop some up on your pointing trowel and press it firmly into the raked-out joints.

❸ Smooth the joint profile into a neat concave shape by drawing an off-cut of garden hose along all the filled joints. Brush away any loose mortar from the brickwork when it has set hard.

Replacing a brick

If the pointing has failed, water can penetrate the brick. If this freezes, the expansion can break away the face of the brick; it is called spalling. The only cure is to replace the brick.

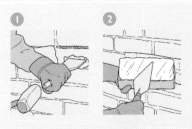

❶ Drill holes into and around the affected brick to make it easier to remove. Then use a brick bolster and club hammer to break up and chop out the pieces.

❷ Chip old mortar out of the recess and spread new mortar on its base and sides. Apply mortar to the top of the new brick as well.

❸ Tap the new brick into place with the handle of your trowel or club hammer. Then trim off excess mortar and neaten the pointing (*see left*).

Repairing render

Many houses have their exterior walls rendered – coated with a layer of cement mortar, which may be smooth or textured or may have pebbles bedded in it (called pebbledash). If the bond with the masonry fails, some repairs will be needed.

you will need

→ pointing trowel
→ old paint brush
→ PVA adhesive
→ patching mortar
→ exterior-grade filler
→ filling knife
→ brick bolster
→ club hammer
→ hawk
→ timber batten
→ steel float

Patching pebbledash

If your walls are pebbledashed, fill the patch as level as you can with your trowel and smooth it off. Then load some pebbles on your hawk and use your float to push them off the edge and into the wet mortar. Press them in well.

Repairing cracks

If there are cracks in the render, but surrounding areas appear sound, you can fill them with mortar or an exterior-grade filler if they are only fine.

❶ Use the tip of your pointing trowel to rake loose material out of the crack. Then brush out remaining debris and apply some diluted PVA building adhesive to help the new mortar bond well.

❷ Mix up some mortar and press it well into the crack, leaving it slightly proud of the surrounding surface. As it hardens, draw the trowel edge along the crack to remove excess mortar.

❸ For fine cracks, press exterior-grade filler into the cracks with a filling knife. If the cracks are deep, you may need to partially fill them, allow the filler to harden, then add more. Smooth off with the filling knife.

Patching holes

A network of interlocking cracks suggests that areas of render have lost their adhesion to the masonry behind. They will have to be removed and patched with fresh mortar. Once you have removed all the loose render, you can repair the damage. Buy a small bag of dry ready-mixed bricklaying mortar for the job.

Mix 1 part PVA building adhesive with 5 parts water and use this to prime and seal the bare brickwork. It will also improve the adhesion of the patch.

Mix up some mortar and place it on a board or hawk. Fill the edges of the hole first, then the centre, leaving the surface about 6mm (¼in) below the surrounding rendering. Criss-cross the surface with your trowel to key it.

Apply a second coat of mortar so it is slightly proud, then use a timber batten to scrape ('rule') off the excess. Move it from side to side as you work upwards so as not to disturb the patch.

Fill any hollows left after ruling off the excess mortar, then wet a steel float and use it to smooth the repair. If the existing surface has a texture, use a sponge or a textured paint roller to imitate it as best you can.

Painting masonry

If your exterior masonry is painted, it will need a fresh coat of paint every few years. This is not a difficult job, just a big one, and the answer is to tackle it one wall at a time. The secret of success is mainly down to having the right access equipment.

Access equipment

Most people use ladders to paint house walls, but working from one for long periods can be uncomfortable. Equip your ladder with a stand-off at the top and a movable foot rest to spare your feet. Add a hook or bracket for your paint container, and a pair of stabilizers to support the foot of the ladder. Set the ladder at the correct angle – the foot should be 1m (3ft) from the wall for every 4m (12ft) of ladder height. Make sure the foot is standing on firm ground or on a levelled board.

Alternatives

If you have hard surfaces all around your house:

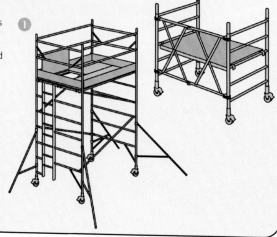

❶ Hire a mobile scaffold tower, which means you can move around the house as you work.

❷ You can also hire low-level platforms that are ideal for work on downstairs walls and single-storey buildings.

Preparation

Clean the wall surfaces to remove dirt, algal growth and other stains (*see page 260*). Use a stiff brush to remove any loose, flaky paint. Fill any cracks and holes in rendering (*see pages 262–263*) and allow the repair to dry.

1 Test painted surfaces with a gloved hand to see if they are chalky. If they are, bind the loose material by brushing on a coat of masonry stabilizing primer.

2 Mask downpipes with newspaper, stuck on with masking tape. This takes a little time, but is worth the effort. Use wide masking tape on the woodwork around windows and doors too.

Applying the paint

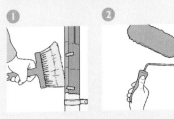

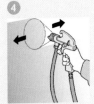

1 On smooth surfaces, apply the paint with a wide brush. Load it generously and brush paint up and down, then from side to side, to get even coverage.

2 On lightly textured surfaces, try using a paint roller with a long-pile sleeve. Load it from a roller bucket hung from your ladder, not from a roller tray. Cut in around any obstacles with a paint brush.

3 On pebbledashed walls, use a banister brush so you can scrub the paint into the surface. Load it from a roller bucket or a large paint kettle.

4 Hire a spray gun with long hoses if you have large areas of heavily textured rendering to paint. Mask all doors and windows completely, and decorate on a still day.

Repairing timber cladding

Timber cladding, also known as clapboarding or siding, is often used as a means of weatherproofing for both masonry and timber-framed external walls. It may be fixed as horizontal (or occasionally vertical) boards, or as individual tiles called shingles.

Repairing shingles

① Shingles are tapered wooden tiles, usually about 400mm (16in) long and often cut in random widths.

② They are fixed to masonry walls by nailing to horizontal battens in much the same way as a roof is tiled, with the shingles overlapping to form a weatherproof surface.

③ A layer of waterproof building paper is usually sandwiched between the battens and the wall.

④ On timber-framed walls, the shingles are normally nailed directly to the timber cladding of the wall panels.

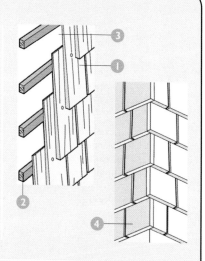

Replacing a split shingle

① To replace a split shingle, use a tool called a slater's ripper (which you can hire) to cut through the fixing nails. Slide its tip behind the shingles, hook it over a nail and hammer downwards to cut through the fixing.

② Pull the split shingle out, and use it as a template to cut and plane the new shingle to size. Slide it up under the course above and nail it through its face to the batten behind its lower edge.

Repairing cladding

Unless timber cladding is regularly treated with paint or wood stain, it can crack and start to rot. Tackle repairs as soon as they become apparent, so that even larger areas are not affected.

❶ Open up cracks in the cladding with a bladed tool, and squirt a generous amount of exterior-grade woodworking adhesive into the open split.

❷ Clamp the crack closed while the adhesive sets by pinning a wood offcut to the face of the board below. Wipe excess adhesive from the crack. Remove the block the following day and fill the nail holes.

❸ Rot starts to affect cladding if the paint film fails and lets water in. Wedge up the rotten board at each side of the affected section and cut through it as far as you can with a tenon saw.

❹ Use a chisel to split out the visible parts of the board. Then slide a hacksaw blade up behind the rotten board to cut through the fixing nails along its top edge.Cut a replacement section of cladding and treat all its surfaces with wood preservative. Use an offcut to tap it into place, then nail through its face into the top edge of the board below.

Painting cladding

Painted cladding is one of the most difficult outdoor surfaces to keep in good condition. Temperature and humidity changes make the boards expand and contract, and this soon cracks the paint film. The best solution is to strip off all the existing paint using a hot-air gun, and to repaint using either microporous paint or wood stain. Both allow moisture to evaporate through the coating, so you no longer get the flaking and cracking that always happens with a traditional paint film. They are easy to refurbish with an extra coat when needed.

Dealing with rising damp

The exterior walls of your house contain a waterproof layer called the damp-proof course (DPC) just above ground level. It is designed to stop moisture rising into the walls from the ground. If it fails, your walls start to suffer from rising damp.

Clearing DPC bridges

The telltale signs of rising damp are extensive damp patches on the interior walls, rising to a height of 1m (3ft) or so above skirting-board level. The cause may be a faulty DPC, but before suspecting this you should first check whether the cause is a DPC bridge – something that is allowing water from the ground to bypass the DPC. Here are some common bridges.

❶ Render covering DPC. Cut away render to above DPC level.

❷ Steps or foundation slabs for outbuildings above DPC level. Insert vertical DPC between the two.

❸ Soil or other damp material against wall above DPC level. Clear away to 150mm (6in) below DPC level.

❹ Outbuilding or garden wall next to house without own DPC. Insert vertical DPC between the two.

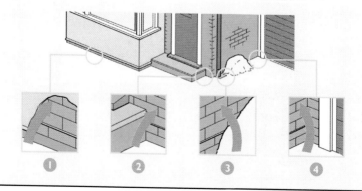

❶ ❷ ❸ ❹

Injecting a chemical DPC

If there is no visible cause of rising
damp, it is likely that the DPC has been
breached at one or more points. In older
houses, the DPC is usually a course of
slates or engineering bricks laid in the
wall, and settlement can cause the
slates or bricks to crack. Newer houses
have strip DPCs of strong plastic, but
these can also become damaged or may
even be dislodged.

❶ You can inject special damp-proofing
liquids into a wall with a defective DPC,
using equipment that is widely available
from hire shops. You drill holes in the
walls at DPC level and insert a set of
nozzles through which the liquid is
pumped under pressure until the
masonry is saturated. You then move
the nozzles along the wall and treat the
next section.

❷ Hire a professional-quality power
drill and long masonry drill bits to do
the drilling; the heavy workload may
burn out a DIY model.

❶

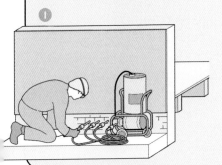

Drilling the holes

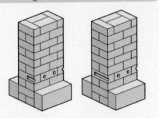

If your house has solid walls, drill the
first set of holes to a depth of 75mm
(3in) and inject the fluid, using the short
nozzles supplied with the machine. Then
drill through the same holes to a depth
of 150mm (6in) and repeat the injection
process, using the long nozzles. This
ensures complete saturation.

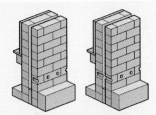

If your house has cavity walls, drill
the first holes to a depth of 75mm (3in)
and inject the fluid, using the short
nozzles. Then drill through the same
holes to a depth of 200mm (8in) and
repeat the process, using the long
nozzles. Fill the holes with mortar
when the job is finished.

Repairing a pitched roof

If you spot a roof tile or slate that has slipped out of place or has cracked, you can fix the problem yourself so long as you have a head for heights and the correct access equipment. If you have neither, call in a roofing contractor to do the work for you.

Safe access

You need an extension ladder and a special roof ladder (both of which you can hire) to work safely on your roof. Set up the extension ladder below the repair area, with its top extending at least three rungs above eaves level. Fit a stand-off (*page 264*) to protect the gutters from damage.

❶ Wheel the roof ladder up the slope until it reaches the roof ridge. It should be long enough to reach down to the eaves.

❷ Turn the ladder over and engage the hook over the roof ridge. Tie its lower end to your extension ladder, then climb carefully on to it.

Fixing a ridge tile

Ridge tiles sit in a mortar bed, and can be dislodged by high winds if the old mortar has failed. Lift the loose tile off and chip away the old mortar.

❶ Carry half a bucket of mortar up to the ridge and set it between the ladder rungs. Spread a thick bed of mortar on the roof along each side of the ridge.

❷ Press the tile down into the mortar until it is level, then trim away excess mortar. Use this mortar to fill the joints at each end of the tile.

Patching roof edges

Roofs with gable ends are often finished flush with the wall below, and the joint between the tiles and the wall (called the verge) is filled with mortar. Chop it out if it is cracked.

Mix up some dry ready-mixed mortar and trowel it into the gap. Finish the repair off flush with the wall below.

Replacing a cracked tile

Tiles have small lugs (nibs) on the back that hook over timber battens nailed across the roof slope. Plain tiles are nailed on at every third or fourth course; interlocking tiles are often not nailed at all.

Drive two wooden wedges under the edges of the tiles above the cracked tile. Slip a builder's trowel under the tile, lift it clear of the batten and remove it. Slide in the new tile, hook its nibs over the battens and remove the wedges.

If the tile is nailed on, use a hired slater's ripper to cut through the nails. Slide in under the tile, hook it around the nail and hammer down to cut it. Replace the tile as above.

Replacing a slate

If a slate has cracked, repair it with self-adhesive flashing tape. Wedge up the slate above and tuck the tape under it. Then smooth down over the crack.

Use a slater's ripper to free the fixed part of a cracked slate so you can slide it out. Then nail a narrow strip of lead to the batten that is visible between the two exposed slates.

Slide in the replacement slate and bend up the lower end of the lead strip to hold it in place. Also do this to secure a sound slate that has slipped because its nails have rusted through.

Repairing a flat roof

The most common type of flat roof on houses is covered with three layers of mineral felt, bonded together with bitumen adhesive and nailed down at seams and edges. The felt can tear at exposed edges, and may be punctured almost anywhere.

Patching a torn edge

Peel back the tear and spray aerosol roof and gutter sealant under it. Wear PVC gloves to protect your hands.

Slip a piece of self-adhesive flashing tape under the tear and press it down on to the felt layer beneath.

Spray more adhesive on top of the flashing tape and press the sides of the tear down into it.

Finish the job by sealing all the edges of the felt and the patch with sealant.

Patching a puncture

If the felt has a visible puncture or has developed a raised blister, a local repair will stop further problems developing.

1 Make two knife cuts through the top layer of felt so you can peel back the four flaps of felt.

2 Spray roof and gutter sealant under the flaps and press them down. Then nail each flap and spray more sealant over the repair.

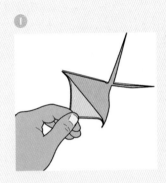

Patching a crack

If the roof has developed a crack across it, repair it with self-adhesive flashing tape. Remove chippings from the area and fill wide cracks with bitumen mastic. Then brush the primer that comes with the tape on to the felt along the split.

1 Peel off the backing paper and stick the tape down along the crack.

2 To bond the tape to the roof surface, tread along its edges all the way along the repair. Then cover it with chippings.

Repairing flashings

The junction between the roof and the adjacent wall will be sealed with a metal or mortar flashing. If this fails, water will penetrate along the edge of the roof. You can also repair this problem with the aid of self-adhesive flashing tape.

1 Remove all loose material from the area. Then brush on the flashing primer an hour before applying the self-adhesive tape.

2 Cut the tape to length, start peeling off the backing paper and press one end into place. Peel more paper as you proceed, then bed the tape in place with a cloth pad.

Fixing gutters and downpipes

Gutters collect rainwater running off the roof and channel it into downpipes, which carry it down to the drains or to a soakaway. They can be blocked by debris and damaged by carelessly placed ladders, or may just rust away with age.

Unblocking a downpipe

❶ If a downpipe becomes blocked, disconnect the top of the pipe from the gutter outlet. Then turn your garden hose on and push it down the pipe from the top. The water pressure and the hose itself should clear all but the most stubborn blockage.

❷ If this fails to work, dismantle the pipe. Work from the top down, unscrewing the pipe clips and lifting each section out in turn. Use a long bamboo cane to clear the blockage, then reassemble the downpipe.

Clearing a blocked gutter

Set up your ladder so you can reach the gutter comfortably, using a ladder stand-off if necessary so that the ladder does not rest on the gutter itself. If the blockage is extensive, be prepared to move the ladder along as you work.

❶ Climb the ladder with a bucket and S-hook, and suspend the bucket safely. Then scoop debris from the gutter with your gloved hand and dump it in the bucket.

❷ Drag your garden hose up to the high end of the gutter and run plenty of water into it to flush away all remaining debris.

you will need

→ basic toolkit
→ garden hose and cane
→ self-adhesive flashing tape
→ roof and gutter sealant
→ wire brush

Repaying a leaking gutter

If the gutter is cracked, seal the damage with self-adhesive flashing tape or apply a bead of roof and gutter sealant with a cartridge gun.

Cast iron gutters often start to leak at the joints because the old sealant has become brittle. Cut through the joint fixing bolt from below with a hacksaw.

Drive out the cut bolt from below with a nail punch and hammer. Then lift out the upper section and use a wire brush to clean both the mating surfaces.

Apply a generous bead of roof and gutter sealant to the joint and lower the raised gutter section into place.

Fit a new bolt and nut through the joint and do it up. Wipe off excess sealant.

On plastic gutters, unclip the gutter from a leaky connector or stop-end (as shown), and check that the rubber gasket inside is correctly seated. Then reassemble the joint.

Putting up new guttering

If you have old cast-iron gutters that are in poor condition, with leaking joints everywhere and an extensive dose of rust, repair is usually not possible or viable. The best solution is to take it all down and fit new plastic gutters and downpipes.

Removing the old system

This is definitely a job for two people, with two ladders and plenty of rope.

❶ Start by lifting out the swan's neck section that links each gutter outlet to its downpipe – it is usually a loose fit. Then prise out the old fixing nails from the top of each downpipe section with a crowbar and lift it up to free it from the section below. Lower it carefully to the ground. Repeat for other sections, then other pipes.

❷ Cut through the fixing bolts between the gutter sections and break the joints apart. Lower each section to the ground with ropes – safer than carrying it.

Setting out the new system

❶ Nail a plumbline to the fascia board 50mm (2in) below the edge of the tiles, above the position of the ground-level gully, and mark with chalk where the downpipe will run.

❷ Fix a bracket to the fascia board at the high end of each gutter section. Run a stringline from here to the nail marking the downpipe position. This will give you a guide for fixing the gutter brackets.

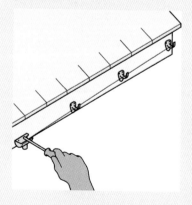

OUTDOORS

Fitting the new guttering

 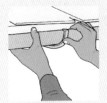

Fit the gutter outlet level with the stringline at the downpipe position. Screw on the other brackets at roughly 1m (3ft) intervals.

Starting at the gutter outlet, clip the first length of gutter into its brackets, rear edge first, and check that it is held securely.

Fit a union piece to connect two lengths of gutter together. Make sure the gutter is correctly seated on the rubber sealing gasket, or it will leak.

Cut the final piece of gutter to length with a hacksaw and fit a stop-end to it. Connect it with a union piece and clip it into the last bracket.

Fitting the new downpipes

❶ Work from the top down. Fit the first length and mark the level of the top bracket on the wall, just below the connector. Drill and plug the holes and screw the bracket on with one screw.

❷ Fit the bracket around the pipe and drive in the second screw. Repeat to add more pipes. Cut the last piece to length above the gully and fit a shoe or pass the pipe through the grating.

Preparing outdoor woodwork

Your house will probably have wooden window and door frames, timber boards forming the eaves, and perhaps other external features such as timber wall cladding. All will need careful preparation before you can redecorate them.

you will need

→ basic toolkit
→ penknife
→ sugar soap
→ exterior wood filler
→ frame sealant

→ paint scraper
→ blowlamp
→ rot repair kit
→ orbital sander
→ detail sander

Doors and windows

Inspect the state of the paintwork, looking for signs of cracks and blisters in the paint film. Use a penknife blade to probe the wood for soft patches that reveal where rot has started to attack.

❶ If paintwork is sound but dirty, remove door furniture and wash down all surfaces with household detergent or sugar soap. Rinse with clean water.

❷ Use exterior-grade wood filler to patch any cracks where joints have opened up, and any small holes.

❸ Key the paint ready for a fresh coat by sanding the surface lightly. Use an orbital sander for flat areas and a detail sander for awkward corners.

❹ Seal any gaps between frames and the masonry by applying a bead of frame sealant with a cartridge gun.

Stripping paint outdoors

If exterior paintwork is badly cracked and blistered, strip if all off, back to bare wood, and build up a new paint system from scratch. Use microporous paint (*see page 281*) rather than a traditional system of primer, undercoat and topcoat; this will not crack or blister and will be much easier to over-paint in the future.

❶ Use a flat scraper and a blowlamp or hot-air stripper to remove paint from large, flat areas such as doors and eaves woodwork.

❷ Use a shavehook for stripping awkwardly shaped surfaces. You will have to use chemical stripper for surfaces next to glass, which will be cracked by a blowlamp or hot-air gun.

Patching rot

You can repair small areas of rotten wood in door and window frames with a rot repair kit. Large areas of rot – in fascia boards or cladding, for example – are best dealt with by fitting new wood (*see pages 266–267*).

❶ Chop out as much of the rotten wood as possible with a chisel. Dry the area with a hot-air gun and brush on the wood-hardening resin in the kit.

❷ Fill the area with the high-performance wood filler in the kit. This sets very quickly, so mix only small amounts. Fill deep holes in layers.

❸ Drill 10mm (⅜in) holes in the wood surrounding the repair, to a depth of about 25mm (1in). Insert a preservative pellet from the kit into each hole.

❹ Fill the holes with the wood filler, and sand the whole area smooth once the repair and the filled holes have set. Apply primer or microporous paint.

Painting outdoor woodwork

Outdoor woodwork generally needs repainting every four or five years.
However, it is a good idea to inspect it every year, and to attend to any
localized areas the paint film has blistered or cracked before rot
can start to develop.

Access equipment

As with painting exterior walls (*see
pages 264–265*), it is essential to use
the correct access equipment – a
ladder with the appropriate accessories
for comfort and safety, or a hired
platform tower where you have good
access all around the house. Steps or
a dual-purpose ladder will be useful
for reaching ground-floor windows.

If you have awkward features, such
as a ground-floor bay window, use
the components of a
platform tower to build
a cantilevered platform
over the top of it.

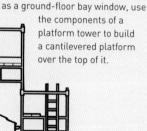

Protecting glass

Nothing makes new paintwork look
more amateurish than a ragged paint
finish around door and window panes.
If rainwater penetrates between the
putty and the glass, it can collect on
the glazing bars and frame members,
encouraging rot to attack. For this
reason, the paint should overlap the
edge of the glass by about 3mm (⅛in)
so it seals the putty-glass junction.

The only foolproof way of getting neat
straight lines around each pane is to
stick masking tape around it before
you start painting. Press the tape
firmly on to the glass, overlap the
corners and trim them off squarely
with a sharp knife.

Don't leave the tape in place for
more than 24 hours after painting,
otherwise it may lift the edge of
the new paint when you pull it off.

Paint systems

If you plan to paint over existing paintwork, your choice of new paint is simple: apply one or two fresh coats of a solvent-based gloss paint in the colour of your choice. Apply a second coat only if the first coat does not give complete coverage – for example, when changing colour. Make sure the first coat is hard dry before putting on the second coat.

If you are spot-painting localized areas where the paint film has failed, scrape away the blistered or cracked paint and sand the area smooth. Touch-in bare wood with primer, then apply two coats of paint over the top.

If you have stripped old paint back to bare wood, or you are painting new wood for the first time, take the opportunity to save time and effort in the future by using a microporous paint instead of a traditional paint system of wood primer, undercoat and top coat. These paints allow moisture vapour to pass through the paint film, preventing the blistering and cracking caused when moisture becomes trapped beneath an impervious three-layer film. Instead, they weather by becoming dusty and dull. When they need repainting, all you have to do is wash down the surface and apply the new paint.

Painting windows

❶ To paint the outside of a sash window, open it and reverse the sashes. Paint as much of the exposed surfaces as possible.

❷ Reverse the sash positions and paint the rest of the exposed surfaces, followed by the frame and sill. Leave the window open to dry.

❸ To paint the outside of a casement window, open it and follow this sequence: start with the exterior frame, then paint the glazing bars, followed by the top and bottom horizontal rails, and finally the vertical stiles.

Painting other woodwork

Eaves woodwork consists of a fascia board to which the gutter brackets are fixed, a horizontal soffit board between the fascia and the wall if the eaves overhang, and sloping bargeboards on gable-end walls. All are flat and easy to paint, although the gutters will prevent you from reaching the whole surface of the fascias. Paint as much as you can conveniently reach. Try to keep paint off the masonry when painting soffits.

Paint cladding board by board, working from the top down. Make sure that exposed ends are liberally coated with paint, but do not over-fill joints or the paint will run.

Painting other surfaces

The outside of your house may have metal surfaces – steel or aluminium windows, for example, or cast-iron rainwater systems and railings – that will need painting. You may also have plastic windows, cladding, fascias and soffits.

Painting plastic

Plastic – usually unplasticized polyvinyl chloride (uPVC for short) – is widely used for replacement windows, and also for wall cladding, fascias, soffits and rainwater systems. It is intended to be maintenance-free. However, its appearance deteriorates with time. Regular cleaning helps prevent dirt from building up, but there will come a time when painting is the only way to refresh the original colour or to change it.

1 Wash dirty surfaces with a solution of household detergent or a special uPVC cleaner (often sold for cleaning plastic garden furniture). Rinse with clean water.

2 On plastic windows, stick masking tape all around to cover the glazing gaskets. Trim the tape to form neat mitres at corners.

3 Apply a coat of special uPVC gloss paint, or of uPVC primer if you are changing colour. Allow this to dry for at least four hours before overpainting.

4 Rub down the painted surface lightly with fine abrasive paper to provide a good key for the final top coat. Wipe away dust with a cloth moistened with a little white spirit.

Painting aluminium

Aluminium does not rust, but develops a white surface coating as time goes by. Remove this using fine abrasive paper and white spirit, then wipe with a clean cloth soaked in white spirit. Prime the metal with zinc phosphate metal primer, then apply a gloss paint.

Painting cast iron

Cast iron is not galvanized, relying instead on a continuous paint coating to protect it from rust. Prepare it for repainting by keying the surface with abrasive paper, then washing it down.

❶ Use a wire brush to remove small areas of rust, then touch in bare metal patches with metal primer.

❷ Repaint by brushing on a generous layer of gloss paint or a rust-inhibiting paint. Work it well into all the crevices, but try to avoid causing runs in the finish.

If years of over-painting have led to an unsightly build-up of paint, you should strip it back to bare metal. Heat is useless for this, because the mass of the metal conducts the heat away before it can soften the paint. Chemical strippers work, but are expensive for large areas. The best solution is to use a coarse wire brush, ideally in a power drill. Wear safety goggles, a dust mask and gloves when tackling the job.

Steel-framed windows

Old steel-framed windows have a coat of galvanizing beneath the paint to protect them from rust. If this coating is damaged, the steel will corrode.

Painting steel windows

Strip paint from rusty steel windows with a chemical paint stripper. Then use a wire brush to remove the rust.

Use a sponge sanding block to rub down the surface of the bare metal. Then clean it with a cloth moistened with a little white spirit.

Brush on a coat of rust remover. Then apply a generous coat of zinc-based metal primer and allow to dry, ready for a coat of gloss paint.

Screen and storm doors

Lightweight screen doors and windows are essential in climates where insect swarms are common. Storm doors and windows are more substantial structures, designed to protect the glass behind from damage during stormy weather.

Mending a damaged screen

Screen doors are lightweight frames fitted with fine mesh screening made of aluminium wire or glassfibre. Small areas of damage can be repaired with patches, but if the screening is badly damaged, it is best to replace it. You will need a special gadget called a splining tool to fit the new material.

you will need
→ screening
→ splining tool
→ silicone mastic
→ basic toolkit

❶ Remove the old rubber spline from its groove in the frame, using a bradawl or a small screwdriver. Save it for reuse if it is undamaged. Wipe the groove.

❷ Lay the new screening over the frame and cut it to size with a knife so its edges overlap the groove by 12mm (½in). Cut each corner diagonally, just inside the outer edge of the groove.

❸ Use the convex roller of the splining tool to push the edge of the screening into its groove. Pull the screening taut as you work your way around the frame.

❹ Use the concave roller to bed the spline in the groove. Do not cut the spline at the corners; instead work it round the angle. Trim off excess screening when you have finished.

Fitting a storm window

Storm windows are custom-built to fit each window. Aluminium types have ribbed flanges to allow them to be trimmed to size.

❶ Apply a bead of silicone mastic around the window frame where the flanges of the new window will make contact with it.

❷ Lift the storm window into position, bed it into the mastic and wipe away any excess. Then screw the window securely to the existing window frame.

Fitting a storm door

Storm doors are also custom-built, and can be hinged at left or right to suit the prevailing wind direction. Screw the door mounting flange directly to the existing door frame, then hang the door, and fit the handle and lock mechanism.

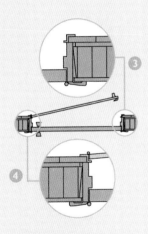

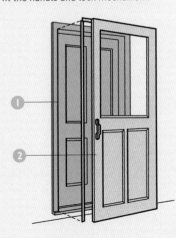

❶ Existing door

❷ Storm door

❸ Detail of door catch

❹ Detail of mounting flange

Patios, paths and steps

Every property has a path leading to the front door, and usually one down the garden. In addition, there may be several other hard-surfaced areas, such as a drive or a patio, and perhaps some steps if the site slopes. All need looking after.

Cleaning surfaces

Outdoor surfaces, whether they are mundane concrete or fancy paving, will benefit from a regular clean-up to remove dirt, stains and the green stuff that makes them dangerously slippery when wet.

❶ Use a patio cleaner to remove general dirt and stains. Dilute it as directed on the container, pour it out and scrub it in with a yard brush. Wash away all the residues with a garden hose.

❷ To clean off more stubborn stains, use a pressure washer. Do not use it on paved surfaces with sand or soil in the joints – it will simply blast the filling out.

Patching concrete

Cracks and potholes in concrete encourage more damage, as water collects in them, freezes and breaks away even more concrete. Fill them as soon as possible.

❶ Cut back the edges of the hole or crack to sound material, using a cold chisel and club hammer. Undercut the edges to help the repair to stick.

❷ Brush debris away and fill the hole with mortar mixed with some diluted PVA building adhesive. Tamp it down well and smooth it off.

Paving slabs

Paving slabs laid on sand can subside, and may be cracked by heavy loads. Lifting and replacing damaged slabs is a simple job.

Repairing paths

The edges of concrete paths, drives and steps are the most vulnerable part of the surface. Repair them before the damage extends farther.

❶ Create support for an edge repair by placing a timber batten alongside it. Secure it in place by driving wooden pegs into the ground.

❷ Mix mortar with some diluted PVA building adhesive and press it into the 'mould'. Tamp it down and level it off. Remove the batten after 48 hours.

Repairing steps

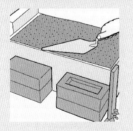

On steps, use bricks to hold the timber mould in place. Fill the broken edge as for a path and leave it to set for 48 hours.

Levelling a slab

❶

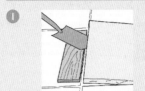

Lever up the affected slab with a garden spade. Use a wood offcut to protect the edge of the next slab.

❷

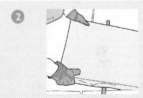

If you cannot lift a large, heavy slab out, slide a broom handle under it and roll it aside. If it is cracked, simply prise out the broken pieces.

❸

Remove any old mortar dabs from the sand bed, level it with a wood offcut and add a little more sand. Slide the slab back into place and tamp it down with a block of wood.

Easy-lay paths

There are several techniques you can use to create a garden path with very little effort or expense. Bark chippings and log rounds are ideal for rustic settings, and gravel is perfect for a more formal garden.

you will need

→ bark chippings
→ preservative-treated boards
→ garden spade
→ garden rake
→ garden roller
→ sand
→ gravel
→ weedproof membrane
→ fence post
→ decorative kerbstones

Using log rounds

If you live in a rural area where logs are plenty, or you have felled a tree in your garden, you can use short logs on end to form a rustic path. Logs about 150mm (6in) long are ideal.

❶ Clear the ground and set the logs on end, as close together as possible. Tamp them down with a fence post to get them all level.

❷ Mix sand and gravel and shovel it in between the logs. Tamp it down well to anchor them in place.

Using bark chippings

Bark chippings are available from garden centres, where they are sold as the ideal mulch for borders. A path needs a secure edge to stop them from creeping into the surrounding garden.

❶ Clear the area for the path and peg stout preservative-treated boards along each edge and at the ends of the path.

❷ Empty the sacks of chippings on to the subsoil and rake them out level with the tops of the perimeter boards.

Laying a gravel path

Gravel is an economical material that is very easy to lay, and is an effective burglar deterrent into the bargain.

> **TIP**
> Order your gravel in bulk from a local builder's merchant.

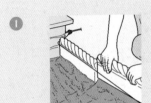

Excavate the area to a depth of about 100mm (4in) and provide a secure edge with decorative kerbstones.

Unroll strips of weedproof membrane over the subsoil to prevent deep-rooted weeds from growing up through the gravel. Overlap strips by 100mm (4in).

Cover the membrane with a layer of sand and gravel to a depth of about 50mm (2in) and rake it out level.

Use a garden roller to compact the sand and gravel layer. If you do not have one, use a fence post to ram it.

Barrow gravel to the path site and use a shovel to fill the area. Rake the gravel out until it is level and is about 25mm (1in) below the top of the kerbstones.

Laying paving blocks

Paving blocks are one of the most popular paving materials for drives, paths and patios. They are small and easy to handle, and are laid quickly on a levelled sand bed. They come in a range of colours and are extremely durable.

Preparing the site

Because the blocks are loose-laid on a sand bed, you need to provide a secure boundary around the area to be paved. The usual way of doing this is to bed the perimeter blocks in mortar on a concrete strip foundation that is a little wider than the blocks.

❶ Lay the strip foundation 48 hours before you plan to lay the paving. Then set the line of edge blocks in place on a mortar bed.

❷ Shovel sand onto the site and level it so its surface is 10mm (½in) less than the block thickness below the top of the perimeter blocks. Use a notched spreader on narrow areas.

❸ On wider areas, lay timber battens on the subsoil and scrape the sand out so that it is level with them. Lift the battens and fill the gaps with sand as you work across the area.

❹ If a manhole is in the way, replace its frame and cover with a special inset version that will contain the blocks.

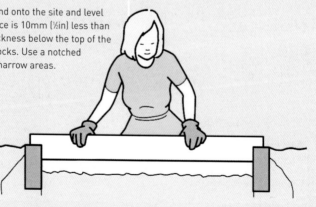

Laying the paving

Place whole blocks on the sand bed at one end of the area. As you progress, kneel on a plank to spread your weight.

When the whole blocks are laid, cut pieces to fit any gaps. Split blocks with a brick bolster and club hammer.

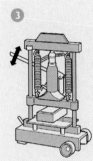

To cut smaller pieces or angled shapes, hire a hydraulic block splitter. Mark the cutting line on the block, place it below the blade and pull down on the handle to split it.

Run a hired plate vibrator over the surface of the blocks to bed them down into the sand bed and compact it so the blocks do not subside.

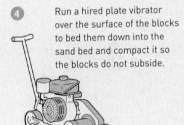

Brush kiln-dried joint-filling sand over the surface of the blocks, and run the plate vibrator over the surface again to work the sand down into the joints.

Finish the job by sweeping off excess sand. You may need to brush more sand into the joints after the first heavy rain falls on the paving.

Laying paving slabs

Paving slabs are squares and rectangles of hydraulically compressed concrete, which can be laid on sand or mortar to create a drive, path or patio. They come in a wide range of colours and textures, and can be arranged in a variety of patterns.

you will need

→ paving slabs
→ sharp sand
→ garden spade
→ garden rake
→ timber beam
→ brick bolster
→ club hammer
→ rubber mallet
→ spirit level
→ long batten
→ mortar for edge slabs

Preparing the site

If your paving will create a patio or path, you can lay the slabs on a bed of sand. For a drive you need a more substantial base (*see pages 294–295*) to support the weight of a car or van, which will crack slabs on a sand bed.

❶ Mark out the area of the patio or path with pegs and stringlines. Then lift turf and excavate the subsoil to a depth of about 50mm (2in) plus the thickness of the slabs you plan to use.

❷ Shovel in the sand, rake it out roughly level, then use a timber beam to scrape and tamp it into a firm, level bed.

Cutting slabs

You will probably need to cut some slabs to complete your paving. You can do this in one of three ways.

❶ To cut slabs up to about 35mm (1⅜in) thick, use a brick bolster and club hammer. Chisel a 3mm (⅛in) deep groove all around the slab, then keep tapping it to open up the cut.

❷ For thicker slabs, hire an angle grinder with a stone-cutting disc. Wear goggles and a dust mask while cutting the slab.

❸ Hire a hydraulic block splitter (*page 291*), which will cut paving slabs as well as smaller paving blocks.

Laying the slabs

❶ Start laying slabs in one corner of the site. Tamp the first slab down with a rubber mallet. Check that it is level in both directions – a slope is not needed on a sand base.

❷ Place the next slab, butted up against the first one, and tamp it down with the mallet. Check that it is level with its neighbour. Add or remove sand from below it if necessary.

❸ Lay further slabs to complete the first row of paving. If you need to kneel on the sand bed, put down a board so you do not disturb the sand.

❹ Carry on placing slabs row by row in your chosen pattern, checking regularly that the paving is level. Set your spirit level on a long batten to span the area.

❷ ❻

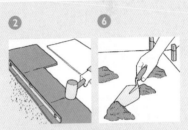

❺ Complete the area by cutting and fitting any part slabs required. Then fill the joints by brushing sand into them.

❻ If perimeter slabs adjoin a flower bed, anchor them by laying each on five blobs of mortar – one beneath each corner and one in the centre. Tamp the slab down level with its neighbours.

Laying a concrete slab

While concrete is unlikely to be your first choice for a patio, path or drive, it is ideal for making a base for an outbuilding such as a garden shed or summerhouse. You need to create a timber mould to contain the concrete while it sets.

Estimating materials

If you plan to mix your own concrete, work out the volume you need so you can estimate how much cement and ballast (mixed sand and aggregate) to order. A small slab for an outbuilding should be 75mm (3in) thick. So a 4 x 3m (12 x 9ft) slab will have a volume of 4 x 3 x 0.075 (12 x 9 x 0.25) = 0.9cu m (27cu ft). To make this, you need 12 bags of 25kg (55lb) cement and 1cu m (35cu ft) of ballast. Order the materials from a builder's merchant and have them delivered. Hire a cement mixer for the day, load it by volume – 1 bucket of cement to 4 buckets of ballast – and add water.

An alternative method that avoids having to order, store and mix materials is to contact a local concrete supplier – not a ready-mix firm, but an operator with a lorry who will mix as much concrete as you need for the job and charge you accordingly. They will also come with barrows, but you will have to provide the labour to move it.

Building the mould

Excavate the site for the slab to a depth of about 150mm (6in), level its base and fill it to a depth of 75mm (3in) with crushed rock (also available from your builder's merchant). Compact it with a garden roller, or use a timber tamping beam, such as an old fence post.

❶ Nail softwood boards to stout pegs to create the mould. Start with one side and get it level.

❷ Set out the other boards, level them with the first one and nail them to their pegs (which must be on the outside of the slab).

Placing the concrete

Dampen the sub-base using a garden hose. Then barrow in the concrete from your mixer and tip it into the mould.

Rake the concrete out until it is a little higher than the formwork. This will allow it to be tamped down level.

Use your shovel to work the concrete into place with a chopping action. This helps to remove air pockets.

With a helper, use a long timber beam to tamp the concrete down level with the formwork. Start at one end of the site and work along it with a sawing motion. Fill hollows with more concrete.

Neaten the edges of the finished slab by running a steel trowel along it, using the edges of the mould as a guide.

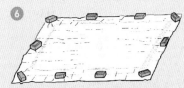

Cover the new concrete slab with a polythene dust sheet weighted down with bricks, so it does not dry too quickly and crack as a result. Allow it to harden for three days.

Decks: the basics

Decks are simple timber structures that provide an outdoor sitting, entertaining or play area. They are an attractive alternative to hard paving, and have the advantage that they can be built easily on sloping sites as well as on level ones.

Choosing the design

The simplest deck is a square or rectangular structure built next to the house wall, usually where there is easy access on to it from the house via patio or French doors. The first step is to plan the size and extent of the deck, which is best done with pegs and stringlines.

The next stage is to plan the structure. On a level site, you need a framework of inner and outer joists that rest on the ground and support the deck boards. To keep rot at bay, the joists may require concrete support pads at intervals under the structure.

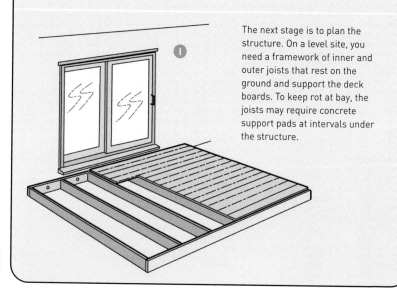

You can then add a balustrade around the deck to enclose it.

The posts are attached to the joists and linked together with a handrail and decorative balusters.

On a sloping site, you need to set support posts in concrete (rather like putting up short fence posts) to carry the deck joists clear of the ground. The deck will need simple steps for access to the garden below.

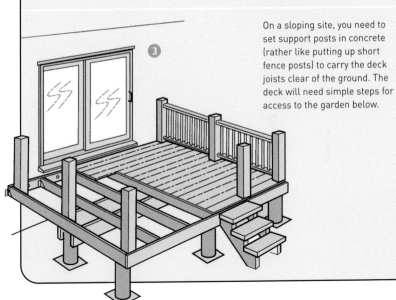

Building a ground-level deck

1

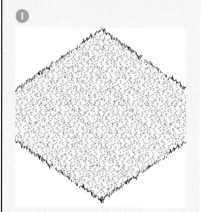

2

3

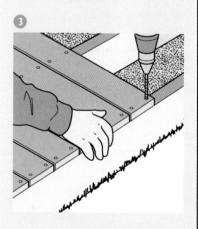

you will need
→ weedproof membrane
→ gravel
→ garden rake
→ joists
→ coach screws
→ galvanized screws
→ decking boards
→ clear wood preservative
  or decking stain
→ basic toolkit

❶ Prepare the site by clearing away turf and excavating to a depth of about 50mm (2in). Lay weedproof membrane to stop weeds growing, and cover it with 50mm (2in) of gravel, raked level.

❷ Cut the joists to size and assemble the framework on the site. Use coach screws (driven through pre-drilled clearance holes) rather than nails. Space joists at 400mm (16in) centres.

❸ Cut the decking boards to length and screw each to every joist it crosses. Use two galvanized screws per board. You can drive them straight in if you use a power screwdriver or cordless drill.

❹ Cut boards must meet over the centre of a joist so each board can be screwed to it. Use loose screws as spacers to place the boards about 3mm (⅛in) apart for drainage.

❺ Treat all cut board ends with a coat of clear wood preservative or decking stain to keep rot at bay.

Decking tiles

❹

❶ If you prefer decking tiles to boards, add extra cross-members to the base frame so that all four edges of each tile are supported.

❷ Then screw the tiles on.

TIP

Consider laying decking boards diagonally or herringbone fashion. Although this means making more complex cuts, the results can be well worth the effort.

Building a raised deck

If you have a sloping site, a raised deck is the perfect way of providing an outdoor sitting area without the need for the major excavation that paving requires. The deck is supported on posts set in concrete, and by a beam on the house wall (known as a wall plate).

Fitting the wall plate

Plan the shape and size of the raised deck as for a ground-level version, and clear the site. Then mark the proposed level of the deck on the house wall. The wall plate that supports the house edge of the deck will be fitted here.

❶ Cut the wall plate to length and drill clearance holes through it at 400mm (16in) intervals to accept expanding masonry bolts. Prop the wall plate in position, level it and mark the wall through the holes.

❷ Replace the wall plate and insert a masonry bolt through it into each hole. Tighten the bolts with a spanner.

Installing the posts

Mark the post positions at a maximum spacing of 1.2m (4ft), and dig a 600mm (2ft) deep hole at each position. Use quick-setting concrete mix, usually sold for fixing fence posts, to secure the posts.

❶ Set each post in its hole, with rubble packing underneath to get its top level with the wall plate, and brace it upright with two battens driven into the ground. Pack concrete in around the post and check that it is vertical with a spirit level.

❷ With all the posts in place, cover the site with weedproof membrane and a thick layer of gravel to keep weeds at bay. Leave the posts to set for at least 48 hours.

Building the deck

Because of the size of the components involved in building a raised deck, it pays to enlist an extra pair of hands to help you with the assembly.

 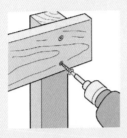

Fix the front beam to the row of posts farthest from the house, so it is parallel to and level with the wall plate. Use two coach screws per post.

Cut the outer side joists to length. Nail a galvanized joist hanger to the wall plate to support the house end of each beam, and rest each joist in its hanger.

 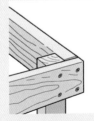

Screw the other end of each side joist to the outer corner post so it butts up against the overlapping end of the outer beam you fixed in step 1.

Cut the intermediate joists to length to fit between the wall plate and the front beam. Fit galvanized joist hangers to the wall plate to support one end, and drive screws through the front beam to support the other.

Decking safety and access

A raised deck needs a balustrade all around it for safety, and a flight of steps to allow access to the lower garden level. The components you need to construct these are all available from decking suppliers.

Fitting a balustrade

The balustrade sections are supported by posts screwed to the main frame of the decking. Each section has a base rail and a hand rail, and the individual balusters are screwed into place before the balustrade section is fitted between the posts.

① Screw the posts to the deck frame at the outer corners and at intervals along the sides of the deck frame.

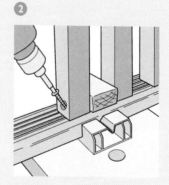

② Cut the base rail and hand rail to length for each section of the balustrade. Clamp the handrail upside down in your workbench and screw the balusters to the rail with screws driven in at an angle. Space the balusters evenly with a wood offcut.

you will need

→ balusters
→ hand rail
→ base rail
→ posts
→ PVA wood glue
→ wooden dowels
→ basic toolkit

TIP

When assembling the balustrade, use quick-release clamps to hold the various pieces in place. Their trigger-operated mechanisms make one-handed installation easy.

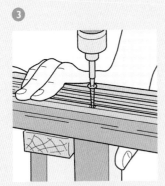

3 Position the base rail on the other ends of the balusters and drive screws through it into each baluster to complete the assembly. Use the same offcut as before to space the balusters.

4 Lift each balustrade assembly into position between its posts and secure it with glued dowel joints. Clamp the assembly together while the glue dries. You may need to slacken or even remove some post screws to allow the balustrades to be fitted.

Adding steps

The simplest way of adding a flight of
steps to a raised deck is to buy ready-
made components – shaped step risers are
available in several sizes, and you cut and
fit treads and risers to suit the layout you
require. Add a centre step riser for flights
over 900mm (3ft) wide.

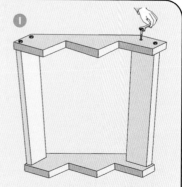

Select the step riser you need and
decide on the width of the flight. Cut
two lengths of deck joist to this width
and screw the step risers to them.

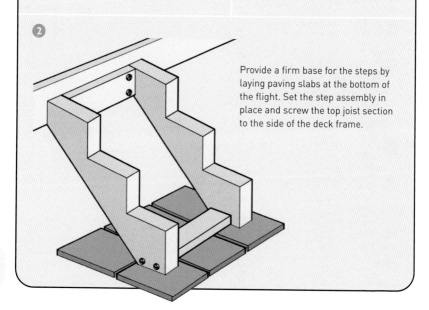

Provide a firm base for the steps by
laying paving slabs at the bottom of
the flight. Set the step assembly in
place and screw the top joist section
to the side of the deck frame.

3

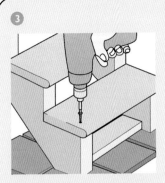

Select the step riser you need and decide on the width of the flight. Cut two lengths of deck joist to this width and screw the step risers to them.

4

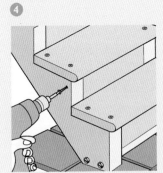

If you want closed steps, fill the gaps with lengths of joist offcut or decking boards. Screw through the step risers into their ends.

Fitting skirting panels

Use fencing trellis panels to create skirting panels for your deck. They will look neat and will prevent large birds and small animals from getting under it.

1

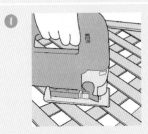

Cut the prefabricated panels down in width with a jigsaw. Prise off the lattice pieces from the frame battens and nail the batten back on to the cut-down trellis panel.

2

Hold the panels in place and screw them to the decking frame. Add further panels to enclose the whole underside of the deck area.

Installing an outside tap

If you want to water your garden or wash your car, you will appreciate the convenience of having an outside tap at the front or back of the house – or both. Installing one means running a branch pipe from the incoming mains supply.

Planning the pipework

• Start by locating a convenient point at which to connect your branch pipe to the incoming mains-pressure cold water pipe above the main stoptap (1). This runs up through the house to the cold water storage tank, and also supplies the kitchen cold tap.

• At this point, you need to insert a tee connector for the branch pipe (2). From here, the pipe then runs to an indoor stoptap (3) (so you can isolate the outside tap in winter) and on to a device called a double check valve (4). This must be fitted to prevent any risk of back-siphonage of water from a garden hose into the main supply pipe if there is a drop in the mains water pressure. Some taps sold for outside use incorporate this valve. The pipe then leaves the house and is connected to the outside tap(s).

• You can use copper pipe for the branch pipe, but plastic pipe is easier and less likely to be damaged by a freeze-up. You can also buy outside tap kits containing all the parts needed for the job.

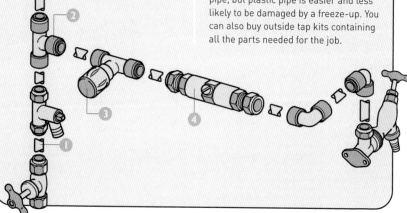

Installing the pipe run and tap

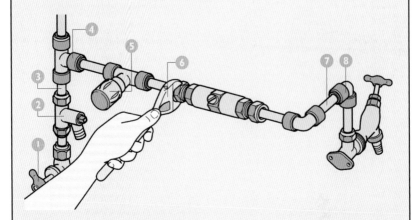

❶ Turn off the rising main stoptap.

❷ Drain the rising main by attaching some hose to the drain valve above the tap and opening it.

❸ Mark the rising main at the connection point and cut out a short section of pipe using a mini pipe cutter (pipeslice).

❹ Push-fit the cut pipe ends into the tee fitting. Then push a short length of new pipe into the branch connection.

❺ Fit a push-fit stoptap on to the open end of this pipe.

❻ Add a further short length of pipe to the stoptap's outlet and connect it to the double check valve.

❼ Drill an 18mm (¾in) diameter hole through the house wall and pass a length of pipe through it. Connect the indoor end to the check valve with an elbow and a short length of pipe.

❽ Outside, fit another elbow and a short length of pipe, and connect it to a backplate elbow. Screw this to the wall. Then wind PTFE tape around the tap thread and screw it into the elbow.

Garden watering

Once you have a water supply out of doors, watering the garden becomes a lot easier. You can connect a hose and use a nozzle or spray gun for hand watering, or use an automatic sprinkler. You should also consider saving and storing rainwater.

you will need

→ one-piece hose connector
→ water butt
→ screws
→ rainwater diverter
→ sprinkler system kit
→ automatic timer
→ basic toolkit

Watering systems

There is more to watering your garden than buying a length of hose and a tap connector. Hose manufacturers now offer a wide range of nozzles, spray guns, sprinklers and other devices that you can connect to your hose to make garden watering quick and easy. Snap-together fittings allow you to connect and disconnect the hose and fittings in an instant. You can even buy metering devices that switch on the watering system automatically.

Consider a sprinkler system

A sprinkler system is ideal if you have a large number of flower beds, saving you a considerable amount of time when watering. You can place the sprinklers so that the water is delivered exactly where needed. A typical system comes as a kit, containing sprinkler heads, valves, connectors and piping, and can be run from an automatic timer. Installation is quite straightforward once you have your outdoor water supply.

Mending a punctured hose

Hoses can develop pinhole leaks, especially if they are left outdoors all year round or misused. They can also be damaged by careless use of garden tools. All you need to repair the damage is a one-piece connector.

 Cut out the damaged section of hose with a sharp knife. Make sure the cut ends are square. Undo the connector and slip a capnut over each end of the hose, then push the connector on to one end.

 Push the other hose end into the connector as far as it will go. Then tighten the capnuts on to the connector to ensure a watertight seal.

Installing a water butt

The simplest way of collecting rainwater for garden watering is to install a water butt, and to connect a rainwater diverter into a house downpipe to fill the butt.

❶ Position the butt and its stand close to the downpipe. Make a mark on the pipe at the same level as the top of the water butt (use a spirit level for guidance). Then make another mark about 100mm (4in) below this.

❷ Use a hacksaw to cut squarely through the downpipe at the marks. Smooth the cut ends of the pipe with fine abrasive paper.

❸ Fit the rainwater diverter between the ends of the pipe.

❹ Use a flat wood bit or a hole saw in your power drill to make a 25mm (1in) diameter hole in the side of the water butt. Fit the connector hose to link the downpipe to the water butt.

Clearing blocked gullies and drains

Your house delivers water into the underground drains in two ways. Downpipes and some ground-floor appliances discharge into gullies, while everything else goes directly into the drains. Both can get blocked, with unpleasant consequences.

Clearing a gully

The gully is the essential connection between rainwater downpipes, and some downstairs appliances, and the underground drains.

1 Downpipe **3** Downpipe shoe

2 Grating **4** Gully

  5 Trap

  6 Underground drain

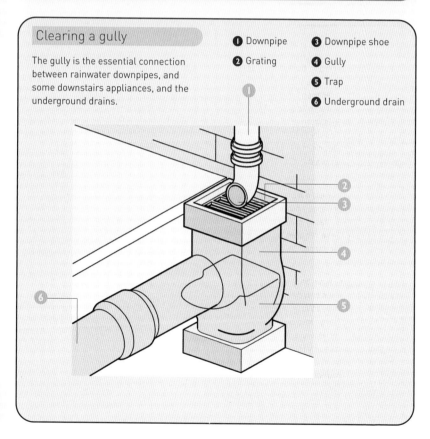

you will need

→ hose pipe
→ rubber gloves
→ bucket

TIP

If your kitchen sink waste pipe discharges above the gully grating, fit a new pipe that passes through the grating and ends above the water. That way, washing-up debris will not block the grating.

• Gullies are buried in the ground, and all you see of them are the small gratings that cover them . Below ground is a U-shaped water-filled trap that stops drain smells from escaping. However, it can easily become blocked by wind-blown debris, and also by grease and other waste from kitchen sinks.

• In older properties, downpipes and waste pipes discharge above the gully grating, which is easily blocked by leaves. Clear these regularly to ensure that water is discharged through it into the gully below.

• Newer homes have back-inlet gullies, and the downpipes run directly into the back-inlet chamber. Waste pipes from the house discharge into a soil stack, not into the gully. However, the grating can still be blocked by leaves, preventing ground water from draining into the gully from surrounding paving. Clear the grating regularly.

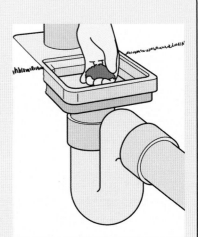

• Clear a blocked trap in either type of gully by removing the grating and scooping out debris with a gloved hand. Flush it through with water from a hose to ensure that it is draining freely.

you will need

→ drain rods (hired)
→ plunger head (hired)
→ corkscrew (hired)
→ hose pipe
→ gloves

TIP

These chambers contain a rodding eye above the trap fitted with a large plug, and this plug may have fallen out and blocked the trap. Only an inspection of the chamber will show if this is the case.

Clearing a blocked drain

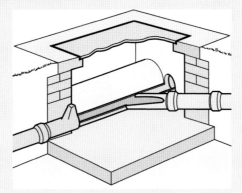

Branch pipes from gullies and from the house's main soil stack connect into the underground drain run at inspection chambers (manholes). These are also installed wherever the drain run changes direction. Water overflowing from a manhole (or from a gully that is not itself blocked) is a sure sign that the drains are blocked somewhere. Lift the covers to assess where the blockage is.

If one chamber is full of water, the blockage lies farther down the drain run. If the next chamber is empty, the blockage lies between the two chambers. If it is full, the blockage lies either between the chamber and the sewer or, in the case of an old-style interceptor chamber with a trap in its outlet, in the trap itself.

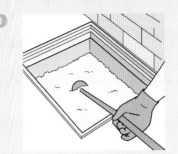

❶ Hire a set of drain rods containing a number of rods plus a plunger head and a corkscrew. Fit the plunger to one rod, then screw other sections together. Feed the rods and plunger into the blocked chamber in the direction of the blockage and try to dislodge it.

❷ Switch to a corkscrew fitting if the plunger does not work. Rotate the rods clockwise as you push them in; if you twist them the other way, they will become unscrewed and sections of rod may become stuck in the drain.

❸ At an interceptor chamber, push the plunger into the trap first. If this fails to clear the blockage, locate the rodding eye and remove the plug so you can rod through it into the drain beyond.

❹ When you have cleared the blockage, flush the pipe through with water from a hose. Dismantle the rods, stand them in the chamber and hose them clean before returning them to the hire shop.

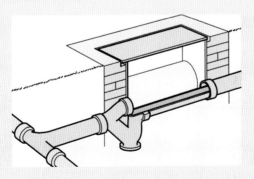

Further reading

There are hundreds of DIY books currently in print, covering every practical and aspirational aspect of the subject. The best source of current titles (and discount prices) is www.amazon.com

If you want a DIY bible on your bookshelf, the big four titles are:

The *Collins Complete DIY Manual*, published by HarperCollins

Reader's Digest Complete DIY Manual

You Can Do It, published by B & Q plc

The *Which? Book of Do-it-Yourself*, published by Which? Books

DIY online

You can also find millions of pages of DIY information on the internet. Type 'DIY' into your favourite search engine and stand back – Google alone has over 7 million pages available! Here are a few of the most useful sites.

DIY stores

www.diy.com (B & Q's site)
www.fads.co.uk
www.focusdiy.co.uk
www.homebase.co.uk
www.ikea.co.uk
www.magnet.co.uk
www.mfi.co.uk
www.wickes.co.uk

DIY tools and equipment

www.axminster.co.uk (mail order)
www.blackanddecker.co.uk
www.boschpowertools.co.uk
www.crownpaint.co.uk
www.dulux.co.uk
www.hss.com (tool hire)
www.machinemart.co.uk (mail order)
www.plasplugs.com
www.polycell.co.uk
www.ronseal.co.uk
www.screwfix.com (mail order)
www.stanleyworks.com
www.woodfit.com (mail order)

Useful conversions

If you're happy working with metric figures, do so – they're generally easier (and therefore more accurate) to use than imperial ones. If you still tend to think in imperial terms, here are some rough conversion factors to use for approximations only.

300 millimetres (mm) equal roughly 1 foot (ft)

900 mm is roughly 1 yard (yd)

500 millilitres (ml) is just less than 1 pint

4.5 litres is roughly 1 gallon

1 kilogram (kg) is just over 2lbs

50 kg is roughly 1 hundredweight (cwt)

1 square metre (sq m or m²) is about 11 square feet

1 cubic metre (cu m or m³) is about 1.3 cubic yards

For precise conversions, use the following with a calculator.

1 in = 25.4mm	1 mm = 0.0394in
1 ft = 305mm	100 mm = 3.94in
1 yd = 915mm	1 metre (m) = 39.37in
1 sq ft = 0.0929 sq m	1 sq m = 10.764 sq ft
1 cu ft = 0.028 cu m	1 cu m = 1.308 cu yd
1 lb = 454 grams (g)	1 kg = 2.205lbs
1 ton = 1016kg	1 tonne = 2205lbs
1 pint = 568ml	1 litre = 1.76 pints
1 gallon = 4.546 litres	5 litres = 1.1 gallons

Index

Acknowledgements

Thanks to Sophie Collins for the *Fix It Good* idea, Rebecca for the execution and Coral for drawing her heart out to illustrate it so beautifully. Above all, thank you to my wife Mary for keeping my spirits up as I wrote it.

Picture Acknowledgements

The publishers would like to thank the following for the use of pictures:

Corbis Jutta Klee 002
Getty Simon Watson cover image